CliffsNotes™

Cather's
My Ántonia

By Susan Van Kirk, M.Ed., and David Kubicek, M.A.

IN THIS BOOK

- ■ Learn about the Life and Background of the Author
- ■ Preview an Introduction to the Novel
- ■ Explore themes, character development, and recurring images in the Critical Commentaries
- ■ Examine in-depth Character Analyses
- ■ Acquire an understanding of the novel with Critical Essays
- ■ Reinforce what you learn with CliffsNotes Review
- ■ Find additional information to further your study in CliffsNotes Resource Center and online at www.cliffsnotes.com

IDG Books Worldwide, Inc.
An International Data Group Company
Foster City, CA • Chicago, IL • Indianapolis, IN • New York, NY

About the Authors

Susan Van Kirk holds a B.A. from Knox College and an M.Ed. from the University of Illinois. She has taught English for 30 years in Monmouth, Illinois.

David Kubicek received an M.A. in English from the University of Nebraska at Lincoln.

Publisher's Acknowledgments

Editorial

Project Editor: Elizabeth Netedu Kuball

Acquisitions Editor: Gregory W. Tubach

Glossary Editors: The editors and staff at Webster's New World™ Dictionaries

Editorial Administrator: Michelle Hacker

Production

Indexer: York Production Services, Inc.

Proofreader: York Production Services, Inc.

IDG Books Indianapolis Production Department

CliffsNotes™ Cather's My Ántonia

Published by
IDG Books Worldwide, Inc.
An International Data Group Company
919 E. Hillsdale Blvd.
Suite 300
Foster City, CA 94404

www.idgbooks.com (IDG Books Worldwide Web site)
www.cliffsnotes.com (CliffsNotes Web site)

Note: If you purchased this book without a cover, you should be aware that this book is stolen property. It was reported as "unsold and destroyed" to the publisher, and neither the author nor the publisher has received any payment for this "stripped book."

Copyright © 2001 IDG Books Worldwide, Inc. All rights reserved. No part of this book, including interior design, cover design, and icons, may be reproduced or transmitted in any form, by any means (electronic, photocopying, recording, or otherwise) without the prior written permission of the publisher.

Library of Congress Control Number: 00-107800

ISBN: 0-7645-8651-3

Printed in the United States of America

10 9 8 7 6 5 4 3 2 1

1O/QY/RS/QQ/IN

Distributed in the United States by IDG Books Worldwide, Inc.

Distributed by CDG Books Canada Inc. for Canada; by Transworld Publishers Limited in the United Kingdom; by IDG Norge Books for Norway; by IDG Sweden Books for Sweden; by IDG Books Australia Publishing Corporation Pty. Ltd. for Australia and New Zealand; by TransQuest Publishers Pte Ltd. for Singapore, Malaysia, Thailand, Indonesia, and Hong Kong; by Gotop Information Inc. for Taiwan; by ICG Muse, Inc. for Japan; by Norma Comunicaciones S.A. for Columbia; by Intersoft for South Africa; by Eyrolles for France; by International Thomson Publishing for Germany, Austria and Switzerland; by Distribuidora Cuspide for Argentina; by LR International for Brazil; by Galileo Libros for Chile; by Ediciones ZETA S.C.R. Ltda. for Peru; by WS Computer Publishing Corporation, Inc., for the Philippines; by Contemporanea de Ediciones for Venezuela; by Express Computer Distributors for the Caribbean and West Indies; by Micronesia Media Distributor, Inc. for Micronesia; by Grupo Editorial Norma S.A. for Guatemala; by Chips Computadoras S.A. de C.V. for Mexico; by Editorial Norma de Panama S.A. for Panama; by American Bookshops for Finland. Authorized Sales Agent: Anthony Rudkin Associates for the Middle East and North Africa.

For general information on IDG Books Worldwide's books in the U.S., please call our Consumer Customer Service department at **800-762-2974.** For reseller information, including discounts and premium sales, please call our Reseller Customer Service department at **800-434-3422.**

For information on where to purchase IDG Books Worldwide's books outside the U.S., please contact our International Sales department at **317-572-3993** or fax **317-572-4002.**

For consumer information on foreign language translations, please contact our Customer Service department at **1-800-434-3422,** fax **317-572-4002,** or e-mail rights@idgbooks.com.

For information on licensing foreign or domestic rights, please phone **+1-650-653-7098.**

For sales inquiries and special prices for bulk quantities, please contact our Order Services department at **800-434-3422** or write to the address above.

For information on using IDG Books Worldwide's books in the classroom or for ordering examination copies, please contact our Educational Sales department at **800-434-2086** or fax **317-572-4005.**

For press review copies, author interviews, or other publicity information, please contact our Public Relations department at **650-653-7000** or fax **650-653-7500.**

For authorization to photocopy items for corporate, personal, or educational use, please contact Copyright Clearance Center, 222 Rosewood Drive, Danvers, MA 01923, or fax **978-750-4470.**

LIMIT OF LIABILITY/DISCLAIMER OF WARRANTY: THE PUBLISHER AND AUTHOR HAVE USED THEIR BEST EFFORTS IN PREPARING THIS BOOK. THE PUBLISHER AND AUTHOR MAKE NO REPRESENTATIONS OR WARRANTIES WITH RESPECT TO THE ACCURACY OR COMPLETENESS OF THE CONTENTS OF THIS BOOK AND SPECIFICALLY DISCLAIM ANY IMPLIED WARRANTIES OF MERCHANTABILITY OR FITNESS FOR A PARTICULAR PURPOSE. THERE ARE NO WARRANTIES WHICH EXTEND BEYOND THE DESCRIPTIONS CONTAINED IN THIS PARAGRAPH. NO WARRANTY MAY BE CREATED OR EXTENDED BY SALES REPRESENTATIVES OR WRITTEN SALES MATERIALS. THE ACCURACY AND COMPLETENESS OF THE INFORMATION PROVIDED HEREIN AND THE OPINIONS STATED HEREIN ARE NOT GUARANTEED OR WARRANTED TO PRODUCE ANY PARTICULAR RESULTS, AND THE ADVICE AND STRATEGIES CONTAINED HEREIN MAY NOT BE SUITABLE FOR EVERY INDIVIDUAL. NEITHER THE PUBLISHER NOR AUTHOR SHALL BE LIABLE FOR ANY LOSS OF PROFIT OR ANY OTHER COMMERCIAL DAMAGES, INCLUDING BUT NOT LIMITED TO SPECIAL, INCIDENTAL, CONSEQUENTIAL, OR OTHER DAMAGES.

Trademarks: Cliffs, CliffsNotes, CliffsNotes, Inc. logo and all related logos and trade dress are registered trademarks or trademarks of IDG Books Worldwide, Inc., in the United States and other countries. All other brand names and product names used in this book are trade names, service marks, trademarks, or registered trademarks of their respective owners. IDG Books Worldwide, Inc., is not associated with any product or vendor mentioned in this book.

is a registered trademark under exclusive license to IDG Books Worldwide, Inc. from International Data Group, Inc.

Table of Contents

How to Use This Book

CliffsNotes Cather's *My Ántonia* supplements the original work, giving you background information about the author, an introduction to the novel, a graphical character map, critical commentaries, expanded glossaries, and a comprehensive index. CliffsNotes Review tests your comprehension of the original text and reinforces learning with questions and answers, practice projects, and more. For further information on Willa Cather and *My Ántonia*, check out the CliffsNotes Resource Center.

CliffsNotes provides the following icons to highlight essential elements of particular interest:

Reveals the underlying themes in the work.

Helps you to more easily relate to or discover the depth of a character.

Uncovers elements such as setting, atmosphere, mystery, passion, violence, irony, symbolism, tragedy, foreshadowing, and satire.

Enables you to appreciate the nuances of words and phrases.

Don't Miss Our Web Site

Discover classic literature as well as modern-day treasures by visiting the CliffsNotes Web site at www.cliffsnotes.com. You'll find interactive tools that are fun and informative, links to interesting Web sites, and additional resources to help you continue your learning.

At www.cliffsnotes.com, you can obtain a quick download of a CliffsNotes title, purchase a title in print form, browse our catalog, or view samples such as a table of contents or a character map quickly and easily. See you at www.cliffsnotes.com!

LIFE AND BACKGROUND OF THE AUTHOR

Early Childhood (1873–1884)

Wilella Cather (rhymes with *gather*) was born on December 7, 1873, in the home of her short, stalwart, maternal grandmother, Rachel Boak, in Back Creek Valley (near Gore), on the northwest tip of Virginia. The oldest of seven children, Willa was named for an aunt who died of diphtheria. She hated her given, or Christian, name and as soon as she had some say about the matter, friends and family knew her as "Willie." She called herself "William" as an adolescent, and she signed her early college papers "William Cather, Jr." Throughout her life—even among family—she insisted that she had been born in 1876.

Willa's father, Charles, was tall and fair, with the manners of a southern gentleman. As a young man, he'd studied law for a couple of years and, because of his helpful nature, neighbors often asked for his help in settling disputes. Willa's mother, Jennie, was the dominant parent, and, according to biographer E. K. Brown, when necessary, she disciplined her children with a rawhide whip; in later years, none of them seemed to resent the whippings and even declared them beneficial. Mrs. Cather, however, gave her children the freedom to do almost anything they wished, so long as they obeyed household rules.

When Willa was about a year old, her parents moved a mile or so to her grandfather William Cather's farm, Willow Shade, named for the multitude of willow trees surrounding the house. The soil at Willow Shade was too poor for farming, so most of the family's income came from raising sheep. Willa enjoyed going with her father to drive in the sheep, just as she equally enjoyed being read to by Grandmother Boak, who lived with the family.

In 1877, Grandfather William and his wife, Caroline, left Virginia and moved to Webster County, Nebraska, where they bought a farm. Six years later, Charles moved his family to join them; Charles' brother George lived on a farm not far away. At first Willa felt as if she were being uprooted from everything familiar to her and abandoned in the middle of nowhere. With no playmates, she often spent her days exploring the vast prairie on her pony, where she discovered German, Norwegian, Swedish, and Bohemian neighbors in their dugouts and sod houses.

In 1884, the family moved to Red Cloud, Nebraska, about seventeen miles away (in those days, the land was open range, and distance had to be estimated by tying a rope with a knot in it around a wagon wheel and counting the revolutions). In town, Willa befriended the town's two doctors, accompanied them on their rounds and learned as much as her eager mind could absorb about prairie medicine. Once, she even administered chloroform to a boy whose leg needed to be amputated. In the evenings, she read to Grandmother Boak from the English classics, the Bible, and *Pilgrim's Progress.*

As a child and adolescent on the Nebraska prairie, Willa Cather grew to know many people, some of whom would later figure prominently in her writing. One of these adults was William Ducker, an Englishman, who began tutoring her in Greek and Latin. The small laboratory in his home fascinated her and she often helped him with his experiments. Mr. Schindelmeisser drank heavily, gave Willa piano lessons, and became the model for Professor Wunsch in *The Song of the Lark.* Mr. and Mrs. Wiener, the Cathers' Jewish neighbors, introduced her to European literature and were immortalized as the Rosens in "Old Mrs. Harris."

Early Formal Education (1884–1890)

Going on eleven, Willa began school in Red Cloud and quickly became aware of how her speech differed from that of her classmates. She worked diligently to eliminate her southern accent. In addition, biographer Edith Lewis reports that "when the other children gave their names at roll call, she hastily improvised for herself the family name of Sibert [her own middle name]."

In June 1890, sixteen-year-old Cather graduated in a class of three from Red Cloud High School. The other two graduates were male and were expected, according to the reporter for the Red Cloud *Chief,* to go on to do great things. All three graduates gave speeches at their commencement, and this same reporter expressed surprise at the power and logic of Cather's speech—an example of her era's belief that rationality and logic were exclusively masculine qualities.

Advanced Education (1890–1895)

In the fall, intent on becoming a doctor, Cather enrolled in The Latin School, Lincoln, Nebraska's preparatory school for students who needed additional science, Latin, Greek, English, or math courses before admission to the university. She rented a small room (which she would later describe in minute detail in the Lincoln chapters of *My Ántonia*) and set to work. Her intense energy and concentration were a dramatic contrast to her parents and siblings, who had a southern, laid-back way about them.

In the spring, Ebenezer Hunt, her English professor, assigned the class a theme on Thomas Carlyle and was so impressed with Cather's essay that he arranged for it to be published, without her knowledge, in the local daily newspaper, the *Nebraska State Journal*. The day it appeared, the undergraduate publication, the *Hesperian*, also published the essay. Basking in the praises of her professor and the editor of the newspaper, Cather decided to forego becoming a doctor. She would major in the humanities and write.

Enrolling at the University of Nebraska, Cather signed up for more Greek and Latin classes, Shakespeare, nineteenth-century writers, German, math, and chemistry. She began to write fiction, acted in plays, worked on the *Hesperian*, and eventually became its managing editor. To the paper, she contributed numerous short stories, editorials, and criticism. Her early work was crude and usually overwritten, and, in later years, well-meaning individuals would suggest that Cather publish it, but she refused to do so, believing that it had no scholarly value.

In the summer of 1893, a hot wind swept over the state, destroying the entire corn crop in three days. Banks failed and people lost their farms. Many families who owed money to Charles Cather, who earned his living by making loans, couldn't pay and he had difficulty supporting his family. Willa's two younger brothers, Roscoe and Douglass, went to work as teachers to help out.

That year, Willa began writing literary and dramatic criticism for the *Nebraska State Journal* at a dollar a column. She enjoyed her life as a newspaper columnist, but it was taxing. She would spend days at the university, evenings at the theater, and the rest of the night at the *Journal*, arriving home at one or two o'clock in the morning. Later, Cather wrote for the weekly *Lincoln Courier*. In time, she developed a distinctive writing style—"meat-ax criticism," some called it—for it pulled no punches. If she didn't like a play, she would say so and tell why in no uncertain terms.

Upon graduation in 1895, she was unable to find a full-time job and asked a friend's father for help. When that hope faded, she returned to Red Cloud and continued to write, mostly short stories. The following year, she was offered the editorship of a new magazine, the *Home Monthly*, based in Pittsburgh. She accepted.

A Career in Journalism (1896–1912)

In Cather's junior year of college, she began growing her hair longer and putting the eccentricities of her early university days behind her. In Pittsburgh, she wore more feminine clothing, and, for the first time in her life, she found herself popular. She was invited to join women's clubs and to attend parties and picnics. She was especially impressed by the museums and concert halls and was happy to be writing prodigiously and earning enough money to support herself. She found it difficult, however, to write magazine copy about the joys of decorating a home and raising children.

When the *Home Monthly* was sold about a year later, Cather resigned and began working on the telegraph desk of the Pittsburgh *Leader*, writing dramatic and musical criticism; she sent the latter back to the *Journal*, in Lincoln. The *Leader* also ran several of her short stories, some under her own name and some under a pseudonym.

Cather's new lifestyle soon began wearing on her. Because many of her columns ran 3,000 to 4,000 words, she was often exhausted. In addition, she was living in cheap boarding houses and eating sparingly and inexpensively so she could send money home to her parents.

While spending a week in New York in 1899, she met Isabelle McClung, the daughter of a wealthy and prominent Pittsburgh judge; this meeting was the beginning of a deep friendship that would last a lifetime. Isabelle admired Cather, who was already a celebrity in town, and the two women shared many of the same interests—theater, music, and art. Not only did Isabelle encourage Cather to write, but, in 1901, she remodeled a third-floor sewing room in the family home as a study for her friend. Cather was delighted and moved into the McClung home.

Launching a short-lived career as a high school instructor, Cather began teaching Latin, algebra, and English at Pittsburgh's Central High School; the following year, she became a full-time English teacher. For a while, she also taught American literature at Allegheny High School.

In the summer of 1902, accompanied by Isabelle, Cather visited Europe for the first time. During their travels, she sent back newspaper articles for the *Nebraska State Journal* to help finance the trip.

In 1903, Cather published a collection of poems, *April Twilights*, and followed it with a collection of short stories, *The Troll Garden*, in 1905. In 1906, she moved to New York as a staffer for *McClure's Magazine* and, in 1908, became the magazine's managing editor. She had ambivalent feelings about her work at *McClure's*. She was thrilled to be working with manuscripts written by some of the world's finest writers—such luminaries as Mark Twain, Kipling, and Conan Doyle—but *McClure's* was increasingly turning to nonfiction, and Cather grew impatient with editing amateurishly written articles on subjects about which she had little interest.

One of these poorly written pieces was a manuscript about Mary Baker Eddy, founder of the Christian Science religion. The manuscript was riddled with factual errors and so badly organized that Cather knew she would have to completely rewrite it. To do this, she had to rent an apartment in Boston to use as a home base while she traveled around New England checking facts.

In Boston, Cather met Sarah Orne Jewett, a writer from Maine, who would become a major influence in Cather's life. Jewett advised Cather to give up journalism and concentrate on writing fiction, but it wasn't until after the publication of *Alexander's Bridge* in 1912 that Cather was confident enough to leave her job at *McClure's* and begin writing full-time. She was later critical of *Alexander's Bridge*, calling it imitative and contrived, and perhaps this is one reason why, with her next novel, she followed Jewett's suggestion and drew on her own background and experiences. The result, *O Pioneers!* (1913), became Cather's first novel about life on the Nebraska prairie.

In 1908, Cather took a small apartment with Edith Lewis (whom she'd first met in Lincoln in 1903) on Washington Place in New York City. Five years later, the two women moved into an attractive seven-room apartment at 5 Bank Street, in Greenwich Village, where they would reside for fifteen years. These would be Cather's happiest and most productive years.

The Creative Years (1912–1927)

Cather's brother Douglass had taken a job with the Santa Fe Railroad, was stationed in Winslow, Arizona, and, in 1912, Cather visited him. From March to June, she traveled through the Southwest, soaking up the legends and history of its Spanish and Indians peoples, and she would draw on these experiences in *The Professor's House* (1925) and *Death Comes for the Archbishop* (1927).

For as long as her family remained in Nebraska, Cather returned to Red Cloud for frequent visits. She loved the prairie and often thought about giving up writing and settling down on a quarter section of land, but always when she was in Nebraska, a sense of loneliness and isolation overwhelmed her and she fled back east.

In 1916, Isabelle McClung married violinist Jan Hambourg. The marriage was as a painful, almost devastating shock to Cather, who disliked change; she felt that she was losing her best friend. In the summer of 1917, the Hambourgs invited her to visit them at the Shattuck Inn in Jaffrey, New Hampshire, and Cather stayed there throughout the summer and fall. Working on *My Ántonia*, the quiet and closeness of nature inspired her, and for many years she continued to work in Jaffrey from mid-September until late November.

Cather's early years as a full-time writer were plagued by money worries. Sales from her first three novels were meager—*My Ántonia* earned less than $1,700 during the first two years after its publication. In 1920, she met Alfred Knopf, who had recently started a publishing company and was deeply committed to publishing quality books. She switched her publishing affiliation to Knopf, giving him the manuscript of *Youth and the Bright Medusa*, a collection of short stories. With Knopf as her publisher, not only did she begin to become better known, but she finally achieved financial security: The 1923 royalties from *Youth and the Bright Medusa* and *One of Ours* amounted to more than $19,000.

As she became more famous, Cather developed an obsession with privacy, giving few interviews and making few public appearances. There are several possible explanations for this public shyness, all of which no doubt were contributing factors: She believed the artist and the person are separate entities, and she was determined to keep her personal life as private as possible and never to be hurt by criticism as she had been at the university; in addition, interviews and public appearances took time away from her work. It was necessary to give a certain number of lectures, readings, and interviews, join literary clubs, and attend literary lunches. These things had nothing to do with literature, she felt, and she cringed at the thought that she might be committed to opinions that she'd told to some reporter a decade before. Before she died, she stated in her will that she never wanted her works to be made into movies or anthologized or published in cheap reprint editions. She also asked that her letters be destroyed.

Cather received honorary degrees from Columbia, Yale, the University of California, the University of Michigan, and Princeton (she was the first woman ever to receive an honorary degree from Princeton). She won the gold medal of the American Academy of Arts and Letters, and *One of Ours* won the Pulitzer Prize.

Last Years (1927–1947)

In the fall of 1927, the apartment building on Bank Street was scheduled to be torn down, so Cather and Lewis took up what they thought would be temporary residence at the Grosvenor Hotel on Fifth Avenue. Because of a string of Cather family crises, however, they were to live at the Grosvenor for five years.

The first crisis came in March 1928, with the death of Cather's father, to whom she'd been very close. In December, her mother, who was living with Douglass in California, had a paralytic stroke and was placed in a Pasadena sanatorium. For two and a half years, Cather worried as her mother grew increasingly feeble. Mrs. Cather died during the summer of 1931, a month after *Shadows on the Rock* was published, while Cather was living on Grand Manan Island. With both parents gone, so died, in a sense, the Red Cloud home. Charles and Jennie Cather were the strong ties that bound the family together, the magnet that kept the siblings returning to Nebraska year after year. That Christmas, Cather made her final visit to Red Cloud. She opened up the old home and stayed there with a former family housekeeper while visiting old friends and family for the last time. The loss of her parents and the breaking up of the Red Cloud home dredged up enough bittersweet memories of her childhood and family to produce two more books: a short story collection, *Obscure Destinies* (1932), and a novel, *Sapphira and the Slave Girl* (1940).

In 1932, Cather and Lewis moved into an apartment on Park Avenue. People criticized her for forsaking her roots, abandoning the immigrants and country folks who peopled her fiction, and even her friend Elizabeth Shepley Sergeant wondered if either Neighbour Rosicky or Old Mrs. Harris, two well-known characters from Cather's short stories, could have gotten past the Park Avenue doorman. But the real reason for Cather's move was seclusion: Her work was being constantly interrupted by the telephone, which she had begun turning off during her working hours, and by people dropping in. She did not have the cold indifference of the self-made woman that Sergeant suggested. In fact, during the Great Depression, she serialized *Lucy Gayheart* for money to help old friends back in Nebraska buy seed and make mortgage payments. She also contributed to a secret fund for the impoverished S. S. McClure, her former boss.

While working on *Lucy Gayheart*, Cather developed a painful inflammation of the tendons in her right wrist. This ailment would plague her for the rest of her life. For months at a time, she would wear a steel and leather brace, which made signing her own name difficult and writing almost impossible.

Throughout most of 1935, Cather cared for Isabelle (McClung) Hambourg, who had become seriously ill with kidney disease. Cather made all of the arrangements to settle Isabelle into a hospital and visited her daily for weeks. When Isabelle died in October 1938, Cather said that she believed all novelists wrote for only one person; for her, this person had been Isabelle.

In April 1938, Cather returned to Willow Shade, in Virginia. She found the countryside drastically changed. The new owner of the farm had cut down the willow trees and destroyed the high box hedges that Cather had loved as a child. The house had so deteriorated that she couldn't bring herself to go inside. These changes, however, lit a fire in her, and she used the energy to complete *Sapphira and the Slave Girl* (1940), her only novel set in Virginia, based in part on her family history.

During Cather's last years, when she was able to do little creative writing, she took more and more pleasure in corresponding with her readers, dictating letters to her secretary. During World War II, Cather and Lewis couldn't go to Grand Manan because most of the workmen on the island were either in the service or working in other industries, and transportation to and from the island became difficult. Thus she set to work on a novel about ancient Avignon. She'd visited the south of France several times, and Avignon had made a major impression on her. After her death, the manuscript was destroyed in accordance with her wishes. She wrote her last story, "The Best Years," for her brother Roscoe, but upon finishing it and preparing to send it to him, she received a telegram informing her of his death.

Although Cather suffered from many ailments in the latter part of her life, she was never an invalid. She rarely let her illnesses depress her, and her mind remained sharp. She died of a cerebral hemorrhage on April 24, 1947, and was buried in Jaffrey, New Hampshire. Engraved on her headstone are these lines from *My Ántonia*: ". . . that is happiness; to be dissolved in something complete and great."

INTRODUCTION TO THE NOVEL

A Brief Synopsis

The novel begins on a train trip in which the narrator and a childhood friend, Jim Burden, share words about the past. Their conversation is a reminiscence about their small hometown of Black Hawk, Nebraska, and a Bohemian girl they both remember named Ántonia Shimerda. Jim has written a memoir about her and the narrator expresses interest in reading the manuscript. Jim delivers it to her, changing the title to *My Ántonia,* and thus indicating that the script will be a personal story. With this introduction, Ántonia Shimerda's story begins and is marked by the changes in the seasons of both life and the prairie.

The reader travels back in time to when Jim Burden's parents die and his Virginia relatives send the 10-year-old Jim to his grandparents, who live on a Nebraska farm. During his train trip, Jim learns of an immigrant family that is also traveling to Black Hawk. When they reach their destination, Otto Fuchs, a cowboy, picks up Jim and Jake Marpole, a hired hand who has accompanied Jim; leaving the station, Jim sees the immigrant family, looking huddled and lost.

Jim meets his kindly grandparents and by the next day he is already appreciating a whole new world of earth, sun, and unending prairie. The following Sunday, Grandmother, Otto, and Jim take provisions to their new neighbors, the immigrant Shimerda family, and find that they are living in a lean-to that fronts a cave. Jim plays with Yulka and Ántonia and agrees to help Ántonia learn English. He also takes his first long pony ride in the autumn colors of Nebraska. But, unlike Jim, the Shimerdas stay close to their farm, believing that the townspeople cannot be trusted, and allowing Ántonia to faithfully see Jim for her English lessons.

At this point there is a side story about Pavel and Peter, two Russians whom Ántonia's father has befriended. On the way home Jim gives Ántonia a reading lesson on a bank near a badger hole. Ántonia explains that in Bohemia the badger is revered; they also rescue a frail green insect, reminding Ántonia of stories from "home." They meet Mr. Shimerda who has killed three rabbits, and he says he will make Ántonia a hat and someday give Jim his gun, a prized possession from Bohemia. His sad smile is a poignant foreshadowing of the future. Ántonia is feeling superior to Jim because she is four years older, but one day when he kills a huge rattlesnake Ántonia tells everyone of their adventure and brags about Jim's role. Now they seem to be more equal. This is only the beginning of their shared memories.

In the fall, the Russians get into trouble with Wick Cutter, Black Hawk's moneylender, and must pay a huge bonus on an overdue loan. When Pavel injures himself while building a barn, Mr. Shimerda, Ántonia, and Jim visit him and hear a grizzly story about why they left Russia. A few days later Pavel dies and Peter sells everything and goes away to cook at a construction camp. Their sad story reflects the harshness of the immigrant experience on the prairie.

Winter comes on and the first few weeks are bitter. Jim takes Ántonia and Yulka in a sled to the Russian's old house. On the way home, the elements are so severe that Jim gets sick and has to stay in with what today is called *tonsillitis*. These weeks are filled with family togetherness, popcorn, taffy, and storytelling. Jake tells Grandmother that the Shimerdas are hungry and living in wretched conditions, so they take Ántonia's family a big hamper of food. A few days later there is a tremendous snowstorm and the Burdens are forced to have "a country Christmas" and stay in with gingerbread cookies and homemade presents. They also send gifts to the Shimerdas. There are prayers and the reading of the Christmas Story from the gospels, culminating with an afternoon visit from Mr. Shimerda. He thanks the Burdens for their kindness and relaxes in the warm, family atmosphere. He crosses himself to pray and, though Jim is afraid his grandfather might be angry because he is conservative in religious matters, Grandfather says that the prayers of all good people are good.

Following Christmas the weather is better and Mrs. Shimerda and Ántonia visit the Burdens. Unlike her humble and grateful husband, Mrs. Shimerda complains that while her family struggles, the Burdens live in luxury, causing Grandmother Burden to give her a cooking pot. Meanwhile, Ántonia tells Jim that her father only came to America because her mother wanted Ambrosch to become rich.

In January, on Jim's eleventh birthday, a blizzard buries the prairie. It is during this time that the despondent Mr. Shimerda commits suicide, putting the barrel of a gun to his mouth and pulling the trigger. While arrangements are made about the body, Jim feels sad for the sensitive man and is hoping that Mr. Shimerda's soul is resting before its long journey back to Bohemia.

The next day Otto returns from Black Hawk with Anton Jelinek, a young Bohemian farmer, who has come to help his fellow immigrants. The coroner and priest arrive and a coffin is fashioned but Mr. Shimerda is denied burial in the Catholic or Norwegian cemetery. Mrs. Shimerda insists that he be buried at the corner of their land where future roads will eventually cross. They inter Mr. Shimerda and years later his grave is a little island with roads curving around it. Jim loves the quiet grave, and in the distant future it is here where he meets and talks with Ántonia.

In the spring, the Shimerdas are living in a new house their neighbors help build and Ántonia is working in the fields like a farm hand. Jim notices that she has become manly and coarse, Mrs. Shimerda remains suspicious and ungrateful, and Ambrosch is deceitful and sly. There is a rift between the two families over a horse collar but it is later healed by Grandfather.

When Jim has been with his grandparents three years, they decide to move into Black Hawk. Here Jim longs for the prairie and misses his friendship with Ántonia and the farmhands. His grandmother arranges for a neighbor, Mrs. Harling, to engage Ántonia as her hired girl. This marks the beginning of Ántonia's experiences in town. She works well for the Harlings, but she is also drawn to a dance pavilion with a group of other hired girls. Among them are Lena Lingard, a dressmaker, and Tiny Soderball, who works at the Boys' Home Hotel. Lena has a dubious reputation and is flirtatious and beautiful. As Jim continues to spend time with Ántonia, by summer her social life is interfering with her job and she is fired. So she goes to work for Wick Cutter, the notorious moneylender and womanizer.

By now a bored Jim is sneaking out at night to dances and seeing Lena who has let him kiss her. He begins to dream sensuous dreams of her but wishes his dream girl were Ántonia. When his grandmother discovers he is sneaking out, Jim is contrite and promises not to do it anymore. A summer picnic is an opportunity for one last idyllic day spent with Ántonia and Lena where Ántonia scolds him for flirting with Lena, telling him he has a greater future than life in Black Hawk. The day ends with a symbolic image of a plow, bold and black against the setting sun.

Meanwhile, Ántonia is suspicious of a trip planned by Wick Cutter and her misgivings prove to be correct. She convinces Jim to spend the night at the Cutters' house and Wick returns in an attempt to seduce Ántonia. She leaves the Cutter employ and once again is engaged by the Harlings.

Jim spends the summer studying for exams to get into the state university. In the fall, he leaves for Lincoln and the university, but no matter how much he studies he finds his life on the prairie and his friendships interfering with his concentration. Lena moves to Lincoln, and she and Jim begin a social life that includes attending plays together, most notably Dumas' *Camille*. This leads Jim to neglect his studies and his Latin teacher, Gaston Cleric, suggests that Jim transfer to Harvard University where Cleric is taking a position. Jim is now nineteen and his grandfather permits him to go to the East. Before he leaves, Lena tells him that Ántonia is engaged to a railroad man, Larry Donavan.

The friends go their separate ways. Jim leaves for Harvard and Ántonia goes to Denver to marry Larry Donovan. Lena opens a dressmaking shop in San Francisco and Tiny Soderball eventually ends up in Alaska where she becomes wealthy. Jim assumes that Ántonia is fine, but he later finds out Donovan deceived her, leaving her pregnant and unmarried. Ántonia returns to Black Hawk, has her baby, and works in the fields once again. On a return visit Jim spends a day with Ántonia and she shows him her baby. She seems somber but settled and Jim tells her how much she has become a part of him. He holds also the memories of her father who lives on in both their hearts. Jim believes this will be the last time they will see each other and he tries to memorize the prairie, the fields, and the tall grass, wishing he were a boy again with a laughing Ántonia running beside him.

Twenty years later, Jim Burden sees Ántonia on a trip to Black Hawk. She has married well to Anton Cuzak, a cousin of Anton Jelinek. They have many children and Jim spends an evening looking at old photographs with them and hearing the stories of the past from Ántonia's children. Meeting her husband, Jim finds that Cuzak already seems to know him because Ántonia has described him so well to her whole family. Happy and contented, Ántonia is rooted in the prairie and the Nebraska farmland. When Jim leaves, he promises to return and take the Cuzak boys hunting the next summer.

Reflecting on the past, Jim realizes that many of his old friends have died or moved away, but he still has memories and longings for the prairie. He remembers the train trip so long ago where he first saw the frightened and small immigrant girl, Ántonia. Now she seems larger than life, like the plow against the sunset, acclimated to the prairie land. In contrast, Jim seems rootless, traveling and adrift in life. He vows to return to the prairie where he felt a peace and contentment that eludes him in the East, and where Ántonia and her family share his past.

List of Characters

The Narrator

Jim Burden gives the manuscript for *My Ántonia* to the unnamed narrator in the introduction to the novel. Because Cather drew many incidents and people in this novel from her own life, her intent in creating this anonymous narrator may have been, in part, to dissuade readers from identifying Cather with first-person narrator Jim.

Jim Burden

He relates a long series of memories about growing up on the Nebraska prairie with Ántonia, a Bohemian girl who seems to embody for him "the country, the conditions, the whole adventure of our childhood." Jim has had many disappointments as an adult, and he glorifies his childhood as the happiest time in his life.

Ántonia (ANN-toe-knee-uh) ("Tony") Shimerda

She arrives at the Nebraska prairie the same night that Jim does, and they grow up together as neighbors. Despite many hardships in her life, Ántonia remains vitally alive and never loses hope for the future.

Josiah Burden

Jim's grandfather—reserved, dignified, and taciturn. Grandfather Burden is "rather narrow in religious matters," but is also generous and fair. He believes that "the prayers of all good people are good." He usually remains neutral in disputes with the neighbors and often serves as a peacekeeper.

Emmaline Burden

Jim's grandmother. Friendly even to the badgers who sometimes steal her chickens, she worries about Ántonia's family, the Shimerdas, although she doesn't wholly approve of them. She inspires confidence; Mr. Shimerda entrusts Ántonia's future to her. When gardening, she is never without her snake cane so that she can kill any stray rattlers.

Jake Marpole

A teenage farmhand on the Virginia farm of Jim's father, Jake accompanies Jim west to work for Grandfather Burden. According to Jim, "Jake's experience of the world was not much wider than mine."

Otto Fuchs

An Austrian immigrant who works for Grandfather Burden. Previously, he lived in mining camps and lost an ear in a Wyoming blizzard when he was a stage driver. He dresses in chaps, spurs, and cowboy boots, and looks like a man "out of the pages of *Jesse James*." For Jim, Otto epitomizes the romantic concept of the Old West cowboy.

Mr. Shimerda

A cultured man, a tailor in Bohemia, and a violin player, he is homesick for the Old Country and can't adjust to harsh prairie life. He is close to Ántonia, and she understands him better than anyone else in the family.

Mrs. Shimerda

Self-centered, grasping, and shrewish, she pressured her husband into moving the family to America because of her ambitions for her son, Ambrosch. Never satisfied with the kindness that her neighbors offer, she always expects them to do more.

Ambrosch Shimerda

Ántonia's older brother—a coarse, vulgar, grasping, self-centered, and irresponsible man with no respect for his neighbors or their property. Whereas Ántonia's values are similar to Mr. Shimerda's, Ambrosch is more like Mrs. Shimerda.

Pavel and Peter

Two Russians who live in a log cabin near a big prairie dog town, Peter is fat and friendly, but Pavel has "a wasted look." He's rumored to be an anarchist because of his "wild gesticulations and his generally excited and rebellious manner."

Widow Steavens

A neighbor of the Burdens, she buys the Burden farm when they move to town. She tells Jim what happened to Ántonia while he was away at Harvard.

Peter Krajiek

The crafty, dishonest Bohemian immigrant who sold the Shimerdas their farm and asked much more for it than it was worth.

Wick (Wycliffe) Cutter and Mrs. Cutter

Black Hawk's moneylender is morally and socially bankrupt. He has grown rich by cheating the townspeople. His wife, angered by his stinginess, paints and sells china to embarrass him. Ironically, he thinks it's amusing. The Cutters' chief pleasure is fighting with each other. Wick finally kills his wife and, moments later, kills himself—in order to keep her family from inheriting his money.

Anton Jelinek

A sympathetic Bohemian from Black Hawk, he comforts the Shimerdas after Mr. Shimerda's suicide. In dramatic contrast to their other countryman, Krajiek, Jelinek is friendly and sincere. He later operates a saloon in Black Hawk.

Mrs. Christian Harling

Mrs. Harling exerts a strong influence on both Jim and Ántonia: "Every inch of her was charged with an energy that made itself felt the moment she entered a room." She hires Ántonia to work for her and teaches her many practical skills. Mrs. Harling makes her household interesting for her children, but when her husband is home, she devotes herself to him.

Christian Harling

A grain merchant and cattle buyer, Mr. Harling is autocratic and imperial. He wears a caped overcoat and sports a diamond ring on his little finger. The household revolves around him; Jim Burden will not go there when he is home.

Frances Harling

The oldest Harling daughter, Frances helps her father in his business. In addition to her exceptional business judgment, Frances has musical talent and is a friendly, outgoing person.

Lena Lingard

Jim Burden remarks, "To dance 'Home, Sweet Home' with Lena was like coming in with the tide." A sensuous, Norwegian immigrant girl, Lena is like Circe in Homer's *Odyssey*, distracting men from their goals. She likes to have fun and plans never to marry. Later, she becomes a successful dressmaker.

Tiny Soderball

A hired girl in Black Hawk, she eventually moves to Seattle and opens a lodging house. She becomes rich in Alaska when a dying prospector deeds her his mine. Like Lena Lingard, she never marries, but unlike Lena, she becomes cynical in later life.

Johnnie Gardener

He owns the Boys' Home Hotel in Black Hawk, where Tiny works. He likes to drink and have a good time, but he realizes he'd be only a clerk if it weren't for Mrs. Gardener, whom he is a little afraid of.

Molly Gardener

The best-dressed woman in Black Hawk, she is indifferent to her possessions. Taciturn and cold, there is "something Indian-like in the rigid immobility of her face." She is the one who keeps the hotel going. The hotel bus is named "Molly Bawn" for her.

Blind d'Arnault

A black musician who plays the piano one night at the hotel in Black Hawk. His music helps make the dull town life endurable for Jim.

The Vannis

One summer, they arrive in Black Hawk and open a dancing pavilion. They keep good order and close on time. Their tent gives children something to do on long summer nights.

Sylvester Lovett

Sylvester loves Lena Lingard but doesn't have sufficient courage to marry a "hired girl," so he marries a widow with property. Jim Burden regards him with contempt.

Harry Paine

Harry, who is to be married soon, tries to kiss Ántonia. Mr. Harling hears the fuss and gives Ántonia an ultimatum: Either she give up going to the dances or else she move out and find work elsewhere.

Larry Donovan

A train conductor and professional ladies' man, Larry courts Ántonia and persuades her to come to Denver on the promise of marriage. He doesn't marry her, spends all of her money, gets her pregnant, and disappears.

Anna Hansen

Always dignified, Norwegian Anna is a hired girl working for the Marshalls.

Ole Benson and Crazy Mary

Ole is a simple, discouraged farmer who has a crush on Lena Lingard. His wife, Crazy Mary, chases Lena with a corn knife.

Mary Dusak

One of the three Bohemian Marys, she is bold, resourceful, and unscrupulous. Her broad face, marked with smallpox scars, is framed with beautiful chestnut hair. The housekeeper for a bachelor, she becomes pregnant with his baby.

Mary Svoboda

Another of the Bohemian Marys, she too has an illegitimate baby. The three Marys are considered highly explosive, but, in time, they all settle down to become thrifty housewives.

Gaston Cleric

Jim Burden's mentor and the head of the Latin Department at the university in Lincoln. Having suffered a long illness while he was in Italy, he came west at his doctor's suggestion.

Colonel Raleigh

Lena Lingard's landlord in Lincoln falls in love with her and gives her a black spaniel named Prince. The southern colonel has invested his money in real estate at inflated prices and cannot understand why his estate value is dwindling.

Ordinsky

A Polish violin teacher, also in love with Lena, he thinks Colonel Raleigh and Jim are compromising her reputation. Finally, he decides that Jim is a worthy friend. He is often wild-tempered, raving about the poor cultural tastes of Lincoln's citizens.

Anton Cuzak

He comes to visit his cousin Anton Jelinek, meets and marries Ántonia Shimerda, and reluctantly becomes a farmer. Homesick at times, he works hard and credits Ántonia for helping make the farm prosper.

Character Map

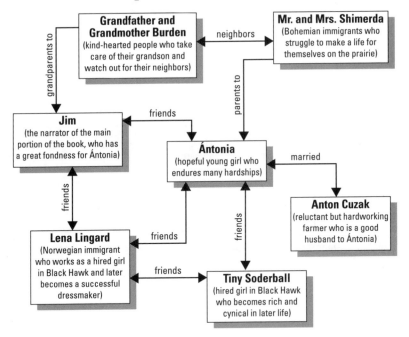

Genealogy Map

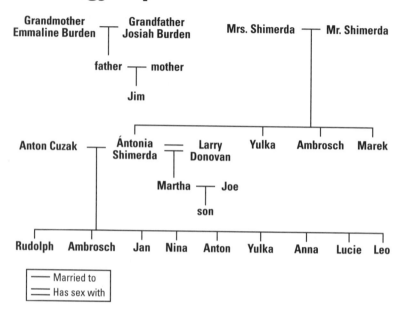

CRITICAL COMMENTARIES

Introduction

Summary

The narrator meets a childhood friend, Jim Burden, now a successful lawyer for a railroad company, while on a train trip crossing Iowa, and they reminisce about growing up in the same small Nebraska town. When Jim says he wonders why the narrator has never written about Ántonia, the narrator makes a pact with Jim that *she* will write about Ántonia if *he* will. (In some editions of the novel, Jim is already writing about Ántonia when he meets the narrator.)

Several months later, Jim delivers his untitled portfolio to the narrator's New York apartment; the narrator has written nothing but a few notes here and there on the subject. After deliberating a moment, Jim writes across the cover of his manuscript, "Ántonia." Then, pausing a moment, he impulsively scribbles another word. The manuscript becomes "My Ántonia."

Commentary

This introduction gives many clues as to what we should look for as we read this novel. The rich descriptions of the prairie suggest that the land will play a major role in the story. Jim's unexciting marriage, how he has been disappointed in life, and his fixation on Ántonia suggest that he was happier as a child than he is now. In this context, note the inscription by Virgil that Cather uses as a preface: "*Optima dies . . . prima fugit,*" meaning, "The best days . . . flee first." The emphasis from the beginning is on loss, especially the brevity of beauty and childhood.

Jim's romantic disposition suggests that, instead of being a strictly objective narrative, this novel will be colored by the narrator's emotions, by his sometimes fanciful interpretations of events. This quality is reinforced when Jim rashly affixes the word *My* before *Ántonia* on his manuscript, making it a personal story, *his* story, about Ántonia.

Book I: The Shimerdas
Chapters I–IV

Summary

After Jim Burden's parents die, his Virginia relatives send the ten-year-old boy to live with his grandparents on their Nebraska farm. He travels by train in the care of teenage Jake Marpole, who was a "hand," a man hired to do chores, on his father's farm. The passenger conductor tells Jim and Jake about an immigrant family on the train whose destination is the same as theirs, and he teases Jim about the attractive girl, near his own age, who is the only one in her family who can speak any English. Otto Fuchs, a farmhand for Jim's grandfather, meets Jim and Jake at the station and drives them out to Grandfather Burden's farm in a wagon.

When Jim awakens, it is afternoon. After a bath in the tin washtub behind the kitchen cookstove, he explores the long cellar next to the kitchen. At supper he meets his bald, blue-eyed, white-bearded grandfather, and that evening he listens to Otto's tales about his adventures in the Far West. Otto answers all of Jim's questions and, in secret, tells the boy about the pony that has been purchased for him. The next day Jim explores the farmyard and goes to the garden to dig with his grandmother, who always takes her rattlesnake cane with her. After she goes back to the house, Jim stays in the garden alone and dreams away the morning, feeling at peace—part of the fabric of the earth, the sun, and the wine-red sea of tall, unending prairie grass.

On Sunday morning, Grandmother, Otto, and Jim take some provisions to their new neighbors, the Shimerdas, who have been living in a lean-to that fronts a cave, eating only corncakes and molasses. While Peter Krajiek translates for Otto and Grandmother, Jim, Ántonia, and Yulka run across the prairie and snuggle down in the tall grass to talk. Ántonia wants to learn English words, and Jim teaches her a few. Later, back at the dugout, Mr. Shimerda gives Grandmother Burden a book containing both an English and a Bohemian alphabet and asks her to teach English to Ántonia.

Jim takes his first long pony ride and is deeply impressed with the rich autumn colors in Nebraska. Over the next several weeks, he takes many rides, exploring the countryside and listening to Otto's stories about the West. Almost every day, Ántonia comes for her reading lesson with Jim; Mrs. Shimerda isn't too happy about this arrangement, but grudgingly she realizes that at least one member of the family should learn English. During those first weeks, the Shimerdas never go to town because Krajiek has made them suspicious of the townspeople.

Commentary

Colored by Jim's feelings and imagination, the first chapter sets the tone of the story. Jake buys young Jim a copy of *Life of Jesse James*, a book which he remembers as "one of the most satisfactory books I have ever read." Jesse James was a romantic figure who became the legendary Robin Hood of the West—robbing from the rich and giving to the poor. Jim illustrates how deeply this book has affected him when he comments that on first seeing Otto Fuchs, "he might have stepped out of the pages of 'Jesse James.'" He goes on to describe him as though Otto were a romantic, reckless character of the Wild West.

As they drive out to the farm through the darkness, Jim feels totally isolated. "There was nothing but land: not a country at all, but the material out of which countries are made." Initially, Jim feels desolate, "erased, blotted out"; not even the spirits of his dead parents are watching over him. His destiny is in the hands of fate.

Jim is especially in awe of Otto Fuchs, listening intently to stories of his experiences and prodding him with questions. Jim compares the prairie country of Nebraska to the sea: "The red of the grass made all the great prairie the colour of wine-stains." This passage suggests Homer's "wine-dark sea" in the *Odyssey* and implies that Jim is on a journey of discovery as was Odysseus. Cather will allude to literary classics many times throughout her novel, as if to remind us that this story has a greater significance than merely being about homesteaders settling the West; its meaning is timeless, larger than any of its characters, and of epic proportions. Jim alludes to the days of Homer and of the Bible, when the world was believed to be flat, when he says "I wanted to walk straight on through the red grass and over the edge of the world. . . ."

In his grandmother's garden, Jim is happy and wonders if people feel like this when they die and "become a part of something entire, whether it is sun and air, or goodness and knowledge." He feels as if he is a part of nature, as human beings originally were in the Garden of Eden before Eve ate from the Tree of Knowledge.

The Shimerdas buy their land from fellow countryman Peter Krajiek, who cheats them because they don't understand English or the value of goods. Mr. Shimerda is neatly dressed and seems to be a melancholy Old World gentleman, whereas Mrs. Shimerda complains about the shed-like house that fronts their cave, and Ambrosch displays interest in the food that the Burdens bring. Only Ántonia seems truly vital and alive, untouched by the hardships.

We see the special relationship between Ántonia and her father when the girl kisses his hand, and when Mr. Shimerda gives Grandmother Burden a book and asks her to teach Ántonia to speak English. Mr. Shimerda has great hopes for his daughter in this new world; to give her a chance at a better life is one of the reasons he came to America.

Jim explores the grassy, treeless prairie. "[T]here were no fences in those days," he says. Keeping in mind that the novel is told from the vantage point of Jim's adulthood, the phrase "in those days" takes on a metaphorical meaning. As a child, Jim had more options open to him; his life could have taken any one of many directions. As an adult, however, his life has been restricted by an unhappy marriage and other disappointments.

Jim recounts Otto's story about the origin of the sunflowers, which he said were brought to this country by the Mormons. Although Jim acknowledges that botanists currently claim the sunflower is native to the plains, the story has taken root in his mind, and in the phrase—the "sunflower-bordered roads always seem to me the roads to freedom"— we can almost detect a tone of regret.

Ántonia enjoys helping Jim's grandmother in the kitchen, and thereby we learn that Mrs. Shimerda's wretched housekeeping is in sharp contrast to Grandmother Burden's careful planning. During their first several months on the prairie, the Shimerdas never go to town, because Krajiek has convinced them that in town they will "somehow be mysteriously separated from their money." They hate Krajiek, but cling to him because he is the only one whom they can easily talk to—and because they don't know how to get rid of him.

Glossary

(Here and in the following chapters, difficult words and phrases, as well as allusions and historical references, are explained.)

badger   any of certain mammals of a family of burrowing carnivores of North America, Europe, and Asia, with a broad back, thick, short legs, and long claws on the forefeet.

Bohemia   a former independent kingdom in central Europe (13th–15th centuries); part of Austria-Hungary until 1918 and then part of Czechoslovakia until 1993, when it was incorporated into the Czech Republic.

box-elder   a medium-sized, fast-growing North American maple, with compound leaves.

catalpa   any of a genus of hardy American and Asiatic trees of the bignonia family, with large, heart-shaped leaves, showy clusters of trumpet-shaped flowers, and slender beanlike pods

chaps   leather trousers without a seat, worn over ordinary trousers by cowboys to protect their legs.

corral   an enclosure for holding or capturing horses, cattle, or other animals; pen.

day-coaches   railroad cars used for daytime travel only.

divide   a ridge that divides two drainage areas; watershed.

draw   a shallow gully or ravine, as one that water drains into or through.

dugout   a shelter dug in the ground or in a hillside.

fire-break   a strip of land cleared or plowed to stop the spread of fire, as in a forest or prairie.

ground-cherry bushes   any of a genus of plants of the nightshade family, including the Chinese-lantern plant, having small tomatolike fruits completely enclosed by a papery calyx.

heavy work-horses   horses used for working, as for pulling a plow.

kawn-tree   Ántonia's pronunciation of *country*.

Mormons   members of the Church of Jesus Christ of Latter-day Saints (commonly called the Mormon Church), founded in the U.S. in 1830 by Joseph Smith; among its sacred books is the Book of Mormon, represented by Smith as his translation of an account of some ancient American peoples by a prophet among them named Mormon.

Prague   capital of Bohemia (later of Czecholoslovakia, and now of the Czech Republic), on the Vltava River.

spurs   a pair of pointed devices worn on the heels by the rider of a horse and used to urge the horse forward.

Tatinek   a familiar Bohemian term meaning *papa*.

windmill   a mill operated by the wind's rotation of large, oblique sails or vanes radiating from a shaft; used as a source of power for grinding grain, pumping water, generating electricity, etc.

Book I: The Shimerdas
Chapters V–VIII

Summary

Ántonia and Jim ride over to visit Pavel and Peter, two Russians whom Ántonia's father has befriended. Pavel isn't home, but Peter is delighted to see them. He shows them around the farm, feeds them watermelon, and entertains them by playing the harmonica. When they are ready to leave, he gives them some cucumbers for Mrs. Shimerda and a lard-pail full of milk.

Jim and Ántonia have a reading lesson on the bank near the badger hole. They discuss the badger, how he is esteemed in Bohemia, and they rescue a frail green insect, which, in return for the warmth of Ántonia's hands, chirps for them. Ántonia is reminded of Old Hata, a beggar woman in Bohemia who dug herbs in the forest and sold them. Children loved to hear the songs she sang in her old cracked voice.

On the way home, they see Mr. Shimerda on the hill where he's been hunting. He shows them the three rabbits he has killed and tells Ántonia that he'll make her a rabbit hat for winter. He says that someday he'll give Jim this gun, which he brought from Bohemia. The sadness of Mr. Shimerda's smile depresses Jim.

Ántonia is four years older and more traveled than Jim, and he resents her air of superiority. Her attitude changes one day, however, when they are on their way home after borrowing a spade from the two Russians. At the prairie dog town, Jim almost backs into a rattlesnake. Ántonia screams at him in Bohemian. He whirls around and kills the rattler with the spade, but he's cross with her for not warning him in English. After this adventure, Ántonia brags about how Jim killed the snake, and she begins to treat him as an equal.

As late autumn lingers, the Russians get into trouble with Black Hawk's moneylender, Wick Cutter, who forces them to pay a huge bonus on an overdue loan and give him a mortgage on their livestock. Later, Pavel injures himself while building a barn. When Mr. Shimerda,

Ántonia, and Jim visit the Russians, thin and emaciated Pavel rouses himself from his sickbed and tells Mr. Shimerda why they left Russia, a story that Ántonia translates for Jim. A few days afterward, Pavel dies. Peter sells everything and goes away to cook at a construction camp.

Commentary

Here, we get our first glimpse of the two Russians, Pavel and Peter. Pavel isn't home when Jim and Ántonia arrive, but Peter greets them jovially, shows them his chickens and his cow, of which he is very proud, and his garden, serves them slices of watermelon, and when they get up to leave, he entertains them by playing tunes on the harmonica because he wants their company. The tunes that he plays are either very happy or very sad. Peter's comment that they left their country because of a "great trouble" foreshadows Pavel's wedding party story later in the narrative.

In Chapter VI, Jim contrasts the end of autumn with the approach of winter. It is a day warm enough to be outside without coats, but as the sun sinks lower in the west, a chill sharpens the air. Seemingly, the insects are all dead—except for this green specimen that Ántonia holds in her hands and talks to in Bohemian because it reminds her of her home in the Old Country. When she and Jim get up to go home, Ántonia puts the insect in her hair and ties her scarf loosely over it. This act symbolizes Ántonia's wish to hold on to summer as long as possible, as well as to hold on to her memory of Bohemia. On the way home, they meet Mr. Shimerda, who notices Jim admiring his gun. In Jim, Mr. Shimerda sees himself as a boy; his promise to give Jim the gun when he is older symbolizes the passing of a legacy from one generation to the next.

An example of Ántonia's maternal nature has always been her protectiveness toward Jim. In order for them to become good friends, however, they must begin to relate to each other as equals. The snake-killing incident serves to cement their friendship; Ántonia is proud of Jim for killing the snake "like big mans," and when they arrive back at the Burden farm, she immediately begins telling the story. Her eagerness to make Jim seem important shows her unselfishness, which is also a maternal characteristic—mothers are proud when their children do well. Jim thoroughly enjoys Ántonia's bragging about him, even though he later realizes that the "big rattler was old, and had led too easy a life;

there was not much fight in him." The snake itself can be seen as a symbol of the complacent settlers who, after having won the battle for their land and built their empires, no longer feel the overpowering need to struggle for survival.

The tale of the wolves, which Pavel unfolds on his deathbed, is another example of Cather's adding depth to the novel by weaving pieces of the Old World into her New World narrative; she used this technique earlier when she inserted the story of Old Hata in the Bohemian forest. The story of the wolves devouring the wedding party serves as a reminder of how harsh nature can be. Cather sets the tone for the story with a description of the onset of Nebraska winter: ". . . a cold wind sprang up and moaned over the prairie," "The wind shook the doors and windows impatiently, then swept on again, singing through the big spaces," "The coyotes broke out again; yap, yap, yap— then the high whine." Jim and Ántonia keep Pavel's story a secret, shared only by them, and this bond draws them closer together.

The loss of his Russian friends weighs heavily on Ántonia's father. While hunting, he goes often to the Russians' empty log house, where he sits and broods until winter forces him to hole up in the dugout.

Glossary

Bohunk   [Slang] a person from east-central Europe; a derisive or contemptuous term.

the bush that burned with fire and was not consumed from Exodus 3, when an angel of God appeared as a burning bush, moments before God revealed himself to Moses.

harness   the assemblage of leather straps and metal pieces by which a horse, mule, etc. is fastened to a vehicle, plow, or load.

He had twelve rattles, but they were broken off before they began to taper, so I insisted that he must once have had twenty-four.   Jim is assuming, as many people do, that rattlesnakes grow one rattle each year of their lives. Actually, a rattlesnake grows a new rattle each time it sheds its skin, which is three or more times a year for a young rattler and once or twice a year for an adult; this makes counting the rattles an unreliable indicator of the snake's age.

lariat   a rope used for tethering grazing horses, etc.

lariat-pin   a peg fixing a lariat to the ground so the animal is restricted to that area.

Prairie dog   any of a group of small, burrowing rodents of North America, having a barking cry and living in colonies.

sledge   a sled or sleigh for carrying loads over ice, snow, etc.

team   two or more horses, oxen, etc. harnessed to the same vehicle or plow.

windlass   a winch, especially a simple one for lifting an anchor, a bucket in a well, etc.

Book I: The Shimerdas
Chapters IX–XII

Summary

The first few weeks of winter are beautiful but bitter, and Jim takes Ántonia and Yulka in a sled, which Otto built, to the Russians' old house. When they start back, around four, the wind has come up, howling across the plains, and the sky has become gray. The girls begin shivering because their clothes aren't warm enough, and Jim gives Yulka his neck scarf, which she forgets to return. Quinsy, an acute inflammation of the tonsils, keeps Jim inside for two weeks after the sled ride, and he reads to his grandmother. On Saturday nights, she pops corn and makes taffy. Sometimes, Otto tells stories.

From Jake's remarks, Grandmother thinks the Shimerdas may be reduced to eating prairie dogs, so she and Jake and Jim take food to their neighbors and are appalled at their wretched living conditions. Mrs. Shimerda reproaches them for their lack of neighborliness, but after Jake brings in the hamper of food, she breaks down and cries.

Mr. Shimerda tells them that they were not beggars in the Old Country. In fact, they have plans for a new log house in the spring, but now the girls must sleep in an alcove dug into the wall of the dugout. Grandmother worries that the Shimerdas don't have enough "horse-sense" to survive on the Nebraska prairie.

Before the guests leave, Mrs. Shimerda gives Grandmother a small sack of something and gives little explanation—except to indicate that it is good to eat. When she gets home, Grandmother tosses the package into the stove, but not before Jim samples one of the items inside; it will be years before he realizes that the sack contained dried mushrooms, gathered "in some deep Bohemian forest."

A snowstorm on the twenty-first of December prevents Jake from going into Black Hawk for Christmas gifts, so they decide to have "a country Christmas," with homemade presents. Grandmother bakes gingerbread cookies, which they decorate with colored frosting. Otto makes candles and fastens them on the little cedar tree that Jake cut from the prairie. They send gifts to the Shimerdas.

Morning prayers on Christmas day are longer than usual. Grandfather reads from the Book of Matthew about the birth of Christ, then thanks the Lord for their food and comfort. He prays for the poor and destitute whose hardships are greater than their own, and a feeling of peace-on-earth pervades the household.

Late in the afternoon, Mr. Shimerda arrives and thanks them for their kindness to his family. After the Burdens ask him to stay for supper, he relaxes in the warm atmosphere. There is an uneasy moment when the candles are lighted on the Christmas tree and Mr. Shimerda falls on his knees and crosses himself. Grandmother fears that Grandfather—who is "rather narrow in religious matters"—will say something, but he just bows his head. After their guest leaves, Grandfather tells Jim that the prayers of all good people are good.

Commentary

In these chapters, we see a stark contrast between life in the Burden household and life in the Shimerda dugout. We also watch Mr. Shimerda sinking deeper and deeper into depression, caused in part by his own observation of the differences between the two households—differences both in material comforts and in the relationships among family members.

When winter descends on the prairie, the Burdens are safe and warm and happy. The Shimerdas, however, are confined to their stuffy cave with only a few provisions; sadly, the few provisions they do have are rotting. Mrs. Shimerda blames the Burdens, whom she thinks should share more of their wealth. But Mr. Shimerda speaks calmly of his plans for the spring. Ántonia tries to explain her family's behavior to the Burdens. For example, to explain Mrs. Shimerda's outburst, she tells Grandmother that her mother is "so sad." When Grandmother is shocked that the girls sleep in a little cave in the wall "not much bigger than an oil barrel," Ántonia maintains that she likes to sleep there because it's warm. Ántonia makes the best of difficult situations, and she hopes for understanding and compassion between the two families.

When a snowstorm forces the Burdens to have an old-fashioned Christmas, members of the family, who themselves have been transplanted to the prairie, contribute items from their own "old countries": colored paper figures from Austria, ones that Otto's mother has sent him during the years, form a nativity scene under the tree, and Jim pastes Sunday School cards and advertising cards that he's brought from Virginia into a book for Yulka.

When Mr. Shimerda spends Christmas day with the Burdens, he seems to be in better spirits than they've seen him in a long time. "I suppose," Jim says, "in the crowded clutter of their cave, the old man had come to believe that peace and order had vanished from the earth, or existed only in the old world he had left so far behind."

Here, Cather states the key problem of all immigrants: the preservation of enough of their household goods and customs so as to make life bearable in a new world. Mr. Shimerda kneels before the Burdens' Christmas tree in reverence to his God, and Grandfather Burden bows his head and Protestantizes the atmosphere, seeing his own notion of God. Each man must preserve his own vision.

Glossary

bobs knobs, or small polished wheels of solid felt or leather with rounded edges.

Bohemie Ántonia is trying to pronounce *Bohemia,* the American name for her country. The Bohemian word for *Bohemia* is *Bohèma.*

horse sense [Informal] common sense.

make up a purse take up a collection.

Mamenka Cather may have misspelled the familiar Bohemian word for *mama,* which is *maminka.*

pommel the rounded, upward-projecting front part of a saddle.

quinsy former term for tonsillitis, inflammation of the tonsils.

Book I: The Shimerdas
Chapter XIII

Summary

A thaw follows Christmas, and the prairie is soon warmed by three weeks of fine weather. Mrs. Shimerda and Ántonia visit the Burdens. Still grumbling, Mrs. Shimerda complains about how her family struggles in poverty while the Burdens live in relative luxury. She snatches an iron pot from the stove and complains that Grandmother has many cooking utensils while she has none, so Grandmother gives her the pot.

Ántonia tells Jim that her father never wanted to come to America; it was her mother who wanted to come so that Ambrosch could become rich. Jim is so disgusted about the pot incident that he doesn't care.

On January 20, Jim's eleventh birthday, a blizzard buries the prairie. Grandfather says that he hasn't seen a storm this bad in the ten years he's lived in Nebraska.

Commentary

Mrs. Shimerda's visit to the Burdens contrasts sharply with Mr. Shimerda's visit in the previous chapter. Mr. Shimerda was happy to be in the Burden home and was thankful for all they'd done for his family; Mrs. Shimerda, however, is jealous, complains that the Burdens haven't done enough, and helps herself to one of Grandmother's cooking pots. Ironically, just as Ántonia and her father are generous and appreciative, so are Ambrosch and his mother envious and grasping.

Glossary

carried in the cobs   brought in a container of corn cobs, to be used as fuel.

The Prince of the House of David   a biblical romance by J. H. Ingrahm, an American novelist.

Book I: The Shimerdas
Chapters XIV–XVI

Summary

When Jim awakens on the morning of January 22, he learns that after dinner the night before, Mr. Shimerda committed suicide in the barn, putting the barrel of his gun into his mouth and pulling the trigger with his big toe. Ambrosch brought the news to the Burdens in the middle of the night and now is asleep on a bench behind the stove; when he wakes, he sits nervously, fingers his rosary, and prays incessantly.

After breakfast, Grandfather, Grandmother, Jake, and Ambrosch leave for the Shimerdas' while Otto heads for town to bring back the priest and coroner. Alone in the house, Jim thinks about what he's learned of Mr. Shimerda's origins. He wonders if Mr. Shimerda's soul is resting here in the Burden home, feeling warm and secure, before beginning its long journey home to Bohemia. Returning later, Otto reports that Ambrosch is obsessed with worry, fearing that his father's soul is in torment. Jim doesn't believe it possible—"Mr. Shimerda had not been rich and selfish: he had only been so unhappy that he could not live any longer."

At noon the next day, Otto returns from Black Hawk with Anton Jelinek, a young Bohemian farmer who has come to help his fellow countrymen. The coroner will arrive later that afternoon, Otto says, but the priest is at the other end of his parish. Jelinek explains how difficult the suicide and the lack of absolution are to the Shimerda family.

Otto begins to build a coffin, and neighbors begin to stop by to pay their respects. Neither the Catholics nor the Norwegians will allow Mr. Shimerda to be interred in their cemeteries. Mrs. Shimerda insists that her husband be buried at the corner of their land, where future roads will eventually cross. Grandfather asks Anton Jelinek if there is an Old Country superstition that a suicide must be buried at a crossroads; the young Bohemian thinks there once may have been such a custom, but he isn't sure. Grandfather declares that Mrs. Shimerda is mistaken if she thinks she will live to see the people of this country "ride over that old man's head."

Mr. Shimerda is buried on the fifth day after his death. Because of the severe cold weather, Ambrosch and Jelinek have to chop into the frozen earth with axes. Before the coffin lid is nailed down, the Shimerdas, in turn, make the sign of the cross on Mr. Shimerda's bandaged head—all except for Yulka, who cries hysterically, afraid to touch the bandage. At the gravesite, the men use ropes to lower the coffin into the hole. Grandfather Burden says a prayer, Otto starts a hymn, and all the neighbors join in singing.

Years later, Grandfather's prediction is proven true; the grave becomes a little island, the roads curving around it. Jim loves the quiet grave because of the spirit of superstition and conciliation that put it there and the spirit of kindness that would not permit anyone in the future to drive over it.

Commentary

Mr. Shimerda's death is the first major turning point in the novel. Ántonia has lost the one person who supported her most; her father was her role model, the family member to whom she was closest. Now she is in danger of coming under the influence of her mother and Ambrosch. In retrospect, we can see Cather is implying that Mr. Shimerda's sadness was caused as much by his feeling of isolation from his family—particularly from his wife—as it was from homesickness. Mrs. Shimerda didn't care about her husband's wants and needs when she decided to come to America; her thoughts were focused solely on Ambrosch. Ántonia was the only family member to acknowledge Mr. Shimerda's sadness; she mentioned it to the Burdens many times.

Cather demonstrates how death has a way of pulling people together: Jim is surprised to see Ambrosch, whom he thought had no feelings for his father, feverishly saying his rosary and praying; neighbors come to visit and offer their support, even though most of these neighbors probably did not make regular visits while Mr. Shimerda was alive. Yet death pushes people apart when the Catholics and Norwegians refuse to allow Mr. Shimerda to be buried in their cemeteries, and these decisions anger even Grandmother Burden, who is able to get along with almost everyone. She exclaims that "if these foreigners are so clannish," she'll get Grandfather to start an American graveyard that is more liberal-minded.

Mr. Shimerda's death is a picture of striking contrasts. He dies in a violent way, but a sense of peace hovers over his grave and will continue to reappear at intervals throughout the novel as a source of strength to Ántonia and as a symbol of tranquility to Jim.

Glossary

a white hart   a female deer; here, a symbol of virginity.

Dives in torment   The reference is to Luke 16:19–31.

victuals   articles of food, especially when prepared for use; pronounced "vittles."

Book I: The Shimerdas
Chapters XVII–XVIII

Summary

By spring, the Shimerdas are living in their new log house, which the neighbors helped build. When Jim rides over to see them, Mrs. Shimerda questions him about what the men are doing in the fields; she thinks they're withholding valuable farming secrets from her family.

Jim is amazed at the change in Ántonia over the last eight months; although she's just turned fifteen, she seems much older. She works like a man in the fields, and Jim feels that she has lost all her refinement. She is proud of her ability to work like a man and tells Jim that she can't start school when the new term begins because she's needed on the farm. Again she talks about how educated her father was and pleads with Jim not to forget him. She asks Jim to tell her about everything he is learning in school. Later, Jim regrets staying for supper because the family seems sordid and materialistic—Ántonia has become coarse; Mrs. Shimerda, suspicious and ungrateful; and Ambrosch, deceitful.

Jim and Jake ride over to the Shimerdas to retrieve a horse collar Ambrosch borrowed from Grandfather. Hesitant at first, Ambrosch finally goes to the stable and returns with a horse collar that looks as if it has been gnawed by rats. Jake loses his temper, which causes Ambrosch to try to kick him in the stomach. Jake punches him, and Ambrosch falls down, stunned. When they see Ántonia and her mother running toward them, clawing the air, they mount their horses and ride away. On Grandfather Burden's advice, Jake goes into town, reports the incident to the justice of the peace, and pays his fine so that the Shimerdas' can't have Jake arrested. Relations between the two families become strained. Grandfather, however, remains neutral, continuing to help the Shimerdas, and Ántonia and Ambrosch continue to treat him with respect.

One day, Grandfather decides to heal the rift and rides over with Jim to ask Ántonia to help Grandmother in the kitchen during the harvesting of the small grain crops. Mrs. Shimerda thinks he's coming to take back the cow that hasn't been completely paid for, but Grandfather tells her she can keep the cow and pay no more. The friendship is repaired, although Mrs. Shimerda remains boastful and taunting, even when she brings Jake a pair of hand-knitted socks as a peace offering.

Commentary

Cather emphasizes Ántonia's kinship with the earth—"Her neck came up strongly out of her shoulders, like the bole of a tree out of the turf"—in strong, masculine, unfeminine language. Ántonia's desire to prove to her mother that she can work as well as Ambrosch leads her to compete with the men in plowing and to pick up masculine traits that overshadow her femininity. Only Grandfather Burden is not worried that hard work will permanently harm Ántonia.

The skirmish between Jake and Ambrosch, as well as the resulting tension between the two families, bring out some new character revelations. Although Ántonia has been portrayed in a positive way, thus far, we now see her with her mother, running toward the two men, plunging through the water without even lifting her skirts, "screaming and clawing the air." Ántonia now has such a strong sense of family bonding that, despite Ambrosch's shortcomings, she is fiercely loyal to him. We wonder if she would have reacted like a wild animal if Mr. Shimerda were still alive. Another revelation occurs when Mrs. Shimerda, normally vindictive and greedy, is uncharacteristically emotional and effusively grateful—kissing Grandfather's hand when he tells her she doesn't owe any more money on the cow and giving Jake a pair of socks she's knitted. It is difficult, however, for Mrs. Shimerda to resist making a final verbal jab about the fight, and Jake, in spite of his quick temper, allows her the last word.

Glossary

draw a shallow gully or ravine, as one that water drains into or through.

sod corn corn grown in a field of freshly broken sod.

Book I: The Shimerdas
Chapter XIX

Summary

July comes on hot and breathless. Jim is kept busy carrying water to the men harvesting wheat. The Burdens enjoy having Ántonia around, even though she clatters pans in the kitchen and runs through the house. Early every morning she goes with Jim to the garden to get vegetables for dinner, and she tells him that she prefers working outdoors to working indoors. As Jim and Ántonia watch a thunderstorm from the chicken-house roof, he asks her why she isn't always nice like this. Her answer: "If I live here, like you, that is different. Things will be easy for you. But they will be hard for us."

Commentary

The novel has come full circle of the year. When Jim and Ántonia came to Nebraska, the potatoes were being dug and the pumpkins lying about the patch; now it is harvest time again. We have seen four seasons: the glorious, peaceful autumn; the bitter winter, with Mr. Shimerda's suicide; the restless spring, with the trouble between neighbors; and, finally, the harvest, with harmony restored. This is symbolic of the circular nature of life with all of its moments of happiness, hopes, promises, and disappointments.

Although Book I ends with a time of tranquility, Ántonia realizes that her life will not always be like this. She wishes she could be more like a man; she feels she needs to be hard to survive and master life on the hard Nebraska prairie. Her final words—"Things will be easy for you. But they will be hard for us."—are like a sinister prediction for more difficult times ahead.

Glossary

hayloft   a loft, or upper story, in a barn or stable, for storing hay.

heat lightning   lightning seen near the horizon, especially on hot evenings, and thought to be reflections of lightning on clouds below the horizon; its thunder is too distant to hear.

Book II: The Hired Girls
Chapters I–IV

Summary

Jim has been living with his grandparents for nearly three years when they decide to move into the town of Black Hawk. Jake and Otto help them move, then they leave and go west together; except for a postcard from Otto, the Burdens never hear from them again. By April, Jim feels at home in town. "I could fight, play 'keeps,' tease the little girls, and use forbidden words as well as any boy in my class," he says. But he is restrained from savagery because Mrs. Harling, the Burdens' nearest neighbor, will not allow him to play with her children unless he behaves. Ambrosch Shimerda comes into town regularly and he puts his horses up in the Burdens' barn, but he never stays for dinner and won't talk about his mother and sisters. News about Ántonia comes from the Widow Steavens, who bought the Burden farm and grew fond of the girl. She tells the Burdens about Ambrosch hiring out Ántonia to work like a man.

In August, when the Harlings' Danish cook leaves them, Grandmother persuades Mrs. Harling to hire Ántonia; then she corners Ambrosch and convinces him that any association with Christian Harling will strengthen his credit. Ántonia fits into the Harling family immediately. Now that she's in town, she learns English so quickly that by the time school begins, she can speak it as well as any of the other children. Ántonia admires Charley Harling, who is slightly older than Jim, because he's always first in his class at school and is mechanically inclined. Ántonia's affection for Charley arouses Jim's jealousy.

In the autumn, Lena Lingard comes to town to learn dressmaking from Mrs. Thomas. She brings news that Tiny Soderball, another farm girl, has gone to work for Mrs. Gardener at the Boys' Home Hotel. After Lena leaves, Frances Harling asks Ántonia why she was not more cordial. Ántonia says that she didn't know if Mrs. Harling would want Lena in her home because Lena has a dubious reputation among her country neighbors. Beautiful, flirtatious Lena drove Ole Benson so out of his mind that his wife, Crazy Mary, used to chase Lena with a corn knife. Through it all, however, Lena remained easygoing and unperturbed. She is determined never to marry and never to live on a farm again.

Commentary

The Burdens lead a more leisurely life in town. An interesting contrast concerns how town life changes Jim and Ántonia. Influenced by his schoolmates, Jim learns to fight, swear, and tease girls. When Ántonia comes to town, however, the roughness of her country life wears off and her "nice" ways return. This change illustrates that Jim is easily influenced by his environment, whereas Ántonia adapts to hers. Recall at the end of Part I, she tells Jim that she must be hard because her life will be hard. When Ántonia comes to town to live in a world more like the one that Mr. Shimerda envisioned for her, her refinement resurfaces.

Cather also contrasts Ántonia with Lena Lingard. Lena is the complete opposite of Ántonia. Ántonia wants a family and hopes to settle down on a farm; Lena wants neither of these things. Ántonia is not overly fastidious about her appearance; Lena wears cotton gloves and takes care not to get her fingers sticky while eating popcorn. Ántonia has a strong sense of what is right; Lena has rather loose morals. Ántonia represents the kind of girl who would make a good wife; Lena represents the sensual girl of young boys' dreams. Like Circe in Homer's *Odyssey*, she leads men astray.

Another contrast worth noting is between Mrs. Harling and her husband. Mrs. Harling is fun-loving, full of energy, and relates well to the children—both her own and the neighbors'. Mr. Harling is strict, demanding, and arrogant. He expects quiet when he is home, and he expects his wife to be attentive only to him. The children are put to bed early when he is home or else they are sent to the neighbors' to play; Jim avoids the Harling house when Mr. Harling is there.

Glossary

ask lief of anybody   ask permission of anyone.

grain elevators   tall warehouses, often cylindrical, for collecting, storing, and discharging grain.

to husk corn   to remove the dry outer covering of an ear of corn.

she went from farm to farm, binding sheaves or working with the threshers   Ambrosch hired out his sister to help farmers with their harvest.

worsted   a smooth, firmly twisted thread or yarn made from long-staple wool combed to make the fibers lie in the same direction.

Book II: The Hired Girls
Chapters V–VII

Summary

Lena and Tiny listen to Anson Kirkpatrick, "Marshall Field's man," play the piano and tell jokes and stories at the Boys' Home Hotel on Saturday nights. Lena tells Jim that she hopes he'll become a traveling salesman when he grows up because they lead such colorful lives. Jim watches Lena help her little brother, Chris, buy a Christmas present for their mother at the dry goods store. Chris doesn't know whether to get a handkerchief monogrammed with a "B" for Berthe or with an "M" for Mother; Lena advises him to get one with a "B"—it will please her because no one calls her by her name anymore. When a neighbor comes in to fetch Chris for the long ride home, Lena watches her brother climb into the wagon and she admits to Jim that she misses her family sometimes.

Winter clamps down hard on the town. Jim spends his evenings at the Harlings' whenever he can because he finds life there more exciting than with his elderly grandparents. When Mr. Harling isn't home, the children listen to music, play charades, make taffy, dance, and tell stories. One evening, Ántonia tells about a tramp who committed suicide by diving headfirst into a threshing machine; she can't understand why anyone would want to die in the summertime.

A pleasant break in the monotony of winter comes one Saturday night when Jim goes to the hotel to hear Blind d'Arnault, a black pianist. The musician has the happiest face Jim has seen since he left Virginia. Blind d'Arnault hears the hired girls—Tiny, Mary Dusak, Lena, and Ántonia—dancing in the dining room, and Anson Kirkpatrick coaxes them to come into the parlor and dance with the men, although Mr. Gardener feels uneasy about this irregularity. Afterward, Jim walks Ántonia back to the Harlings, and they stand talking outside the front gate until the cold chills the restlessness out of them.

Commentary

The country people are isolated, but town dwellers have easy access to the outside world. Traveling salesmen come in by train every weekend, and they gather at the Boys' Home Hotel to listen to music and tell stories. The trains also bring musicians such as Blind d'Arnault. The townspeople enjoy news and culture by traveling only a short distance from home, whereas country people, who would have to journey for miles, are cut off from these luxuries. Notice that winter does not deprive Jim and the girls of a night out, but remember that when they were living on the farm, the Burdens had a homemade Christmas because a blizzard kept Jake from going to town to shop.

In this section, we learn that Lena is not as artificial and shallow as she at first appeared to be. She counsels Chris to buy the handkerchief with their mother's initial on it because it will please her, and she confides in Jim that she misses her family. This is proof that underneath her china-doll facade, she is warmhearted and sensitive. We also learn something of the Lingard family; little Chris, who works at a cold, hard job and desperately needs an overcoat, shows his generosity when he spends his money on Christmas presents for his mother and six younger siblings.

In this section, Cather contrasts the cold outside with the warmth inside in several ways. For example, note how the children, hungry for beauty, huddle outside the Methodist Church to watch the crude blues and reds in the stained glass windows. Another example of a pocket of warmth amidst the cold of winter is the circle of camaraderie in the Harling home. In addition, the dreariness of winter is relieved by the appearance of Blind d'Arnault. Nearly every color adjective used to describe this man is related to yellow, a warm color: yellow fingers, gold watch, topaz ring, yellow man, and a gold-headed cane. He is also called an "African god of pleasure, full of strong, savage blood." The cold drabness of winter serves as backdrop against which shines the brilliance of d'Arnault and his emotional piano performance.

We are reminded of Jim's southern background when he comments that Blind d'Arnault's face is the happiest he has seen since he left Virginia. We are also reminded of the newness of the small-town atmosphere of Black Hawk. In one sentence, Cather calls to mind much that has already happened in the story.

Glossary

Booth and Barrett Edwin Booth (1833–1893) and John Barrett (1838–1891), two prominent nineteenth-century Shakespearean actors, formed a theatrical troupe in 1887 and traveled around the country putting on dramatic productions.

Buying "findings" for Mrs. Thomas Findings are small articles used in various trades; in the case of Mrs. Thomas, a dressmaker, these would be buttons, hooks, fringe, and the like.

cinders any matter, as coal or wood, burned out or partly burned, but not reduced to ashes.

cut bands cutting pieces of twine or metal to be used for binding sheaves of grain.

commercial travellers traveling salesmen.

Get your back up an order to show some courage. Anson Kirkpatrick says this to Johnnie Gardener, who worries that his wife won't like it when she hears that the hired girls have been dancing with the men who are staying at the hotel.

Marshall Field's man a salesman representing Marshall Field's large retail dry-goods store in Chicago.

Mary Anderson an actress (1859–1940) who was noted for her beauty and her flexible voice. She retired from the stage in 1889 after suffering a nervous collapse during a performance in Washington, D.C.

"retail trade" a customer, rather than a retail merchant, who is purchasing items for resale.

the spirit if not the fact of slavery persisted Although slavery was illegal, many white people treated blacks as inferiors and denied them rights and courtesies that they themselves expected.

threshing the act of freeing grain or seed from hulls.

Book II: The Hired Girls
Chapters VIII–X

Summary

In June, four Italians—the Vannis—arrive in town and set up a dancing pavilion. Dancing becomes the trend this summer, just as roller skating was the trend last summer. Parents send their children to take dancing lessons from the Vannis. On Saturday evenings, the local boys go to the dance pavilion, risking "a tiff with their sweethearts and general condemnation for a waltz with 'the hired girls.'"

Jim explains that the foreign girls from the country are hired out in town so that they can give financial help to their large families on the farm. Because the daughters of Black Hawk townspeople are not used to doing physical labor, they have "a confident, unenquiring belief that they [are] 'refined,' and that the country girls, who 'worked out,' [are] not." Jim remembers the foreign girls having a zest for life that made them attractive to the local boys, but like Sylvester Lovett, who is infatuated with Lena Lingard, the boys who live in town don't have the courage to marry the hired girls. This flaw outrages Jim.

Ántonia becomes extremely popular with the town boys at the Vannis' tent, and her social life soon begins to interfere with her domestic work at the Harlings'. One night, Harry Paine, who is engaged to be married in two days, walks her home. When he tries to kiss her, she slaps him. Mr. Harling hears the commotion and gives Ántonia an ultimatum: Either she must quit going to the dances or else she will have to find another position. She decides to go to work for the Cutters, even though Mrs. Harling warns her that it will be her ruin.

Commentary

Cather reminds us again of the changing seasons and the ticking of the clock. To mark the passage of time, the author uses such words as these: weeks, all day, every morning, every day, every evening, as well as such phrases as "sat on the shady side," "lounged in the sun," "sit out in the grass plot," "sat like images," and "our feet hurried." This last phrase is symbolic; their feet are hurrying toward adulthood. Jim lets us know that he is conscious of his youth slipping away when he says that boys and girls are growing up, and "life can't stand still, not even in the quietest country towns; and they have to grow up, whether they will or no."

Literary Device

In her description of Mrs. Vanni, Cather uses color to communicate the air of excitement surrounding this woman: Mrs. Vanni wears "lavender with a great deal of black lace," and "red coral combs" in her hair. In addition, she has an "important watch-chain lying on her bosom." Jim is glad that the dance pavilion is in town; since moving to Black Hawk, he has been desperately searching for activities to replace the active life he led on the farm.

As an adult, Jim is contemptuous of the attitude of the townspeople in Black Hawk, those who felt superior toward the foreign, hired girls, but he doesn't seem to realize that he did the same thing—that is, he left Black Hawk and married someone with money, someone who wasn't a first- or second-generation immigrant. Remember, this story is being told by the *adult* Jim Burden looking back on his youth.

Perhaps it is inevitable that Mr. Harling and Ántonia eventually clash. Mr. Harling is an authoritarian; he is accustomed to being obeyed. Ántonia is an individualistic free spirit who doesn't like restrictions. When given an ultimatum to stop going to the dances or find another job, she makes her decision easily: She will leave the Harlings and go to work for the Cutters. The Cutters have no children to look after, and there will be less work to do; Ántonia will have more time to enjoy life.

Glossary

brood-sow   a sow kept for breeding.

elder   any of a group of shrubs and small trees of the honeysuckle family, with compound leaves and flat-topped clusters of small white flowers followed by red or purple berries.

fancy-work   needlework, tailoring, stitchery.

parasol   a lightweight umbrella carried by women as a sunshade.

dray   a low, sturdily built cart with detachable sides, for carrying heavy loads.

pavilion   a large tent, usually with a peaked top.

plough   a farm implement used to cut, turn up, and break up the soil.

Progressive Euchre Club   a club for playing euchre, a card game basically for two, three, or four players, played with thirty-two cards (sevens up through aces), five cards being dealt to each player.

reaper   a machine for cutting grain.

steer   a castrated male ox, especially one raised for beef.

Book II: The Hired Girls
Chapters XI–XV

Summary

Living at the Cutters', Ántonia has more time to spend with Lena, Tiny, and Norwegian Anna. One afternoon, the girls tease Jim about his grandmother's hope that he become a Baptist preacher when he grows up. Because Jim shows no interest in Black Hawk's young girls and prefers the older, hired girls' company, the townspeople begin to whisper among themselves that there must be something strange about him.

Jim discovers that he can't go to the Harlings' in the evenings; Mrs. Harling is cool to him because he is still associating with Ántonia. In desperation, he searches for something interesting to do, but every place he goes is dull, and everyone he talks to seems to be scheming for ways to get out of this small town because they too are bored. For a while, Jim goes to Anton Jelinek's saloon to listen to the talk, but Anton knows that Grandfather Burden doesn't approve, so he asks Jim not to come in any more.

Jim prefers the dances at the Firemen's Hall, where the hired girls go, rather than the dances at the Masonic Hall, where the so-called respectable young townspeople socialize. He knows his grandparents would disapprove, so he has to sneak out in order to attend. One night Jim walks Ántonia home. When he tries to kiss her passionately, she scolds him. Defensively, he tells her that Lena has let him kiss her like that. She warns him not to make a fool of himself like the other Black Hawk boys because he's going away to school to make something of himself. That night Jim dreams of Lena coming to him—sensuously, reaping hook in hand—across a harvested field. On waking, he wishes he could have the same dream about Ántonia.

Grandmother Burden learns that Jim has been sneaking out to dances, and she is so grieved that the boy stops going altogether. He's surprised to realize that he really is hurt by the townspeople's talk about him. He feels lonely and shut out and spends many spring hours reading

Latin so he can do well when he enters college in the fall. At his high school graduation, Jim gives a stirring speech that surprises and pleases Mrs. Harling. Ántonia, Lena, and Anna congratulate him, too. He tells Ántonia that he was thinking of her father when he wrote the speech. She cries and hugs him, and he feels that her pleasure is his greatest triumph.

When he arrives for a summer picnic at the river with the hired girls, he finds Ántonia crying because the elder flowers remind her of Bohemia. She tells him about the Old Country and reveals that her father married her mother—against his family's wishes—because she was pregnant with his child. Jim tells her of the intensity he sensed when he was left alone after his grandparents went to see Ántonia's father's body; he is sure that her father's spirit stopped to rest at the Burden farm before starting its journey home to his native land. His words comfort her. When Lena, Tiny, and Anna return to the riverbank, they talk about their families and how difficult it has been for them to adapt to life on the plains. Jim tells them the story of Coronado and his search for the Seven Golden Cities. Late in the day, as the sun is going down in the distance, they see the silhouette of a plow, bold and black, against the setting sun; then, just as quickly, it vanishes as the sun drops below the horizon.

One day, the Cutters go to Omaha. Ántonia tells Grandmother Burden how strange Mr. Cutter acted, storing valuables under her bed and insisting that she promise to sleep there alone. Grandmother is apprehensive. She persuades Jim to sleep at the Cutters' while Ántonia sleeps at the Burden home. Cutter returns home unexpectedly in the middle of the night and, in the dark, begins caressing Jim in the bed where he hoped to find Ántonia. Enraged, he attacks the boy and accuses him of having an affair with Ántonia. Jim scrambles out the window and dashes home, bruised and lacerated. He's furious with Ántonia for putting him in a situation that could make him a laughingstock if word ever leaked out. Ántonia decides to return to her family on the farm for a while, and Grandmother accompanies her to the Cutters' to pack her trunk. While they are there, the irate Mrs. Cutter returns, and Grandmother learns that Mr. Cutter tricked his wife into boarding the wrong train, one bound for Kansas City, so he could come back a day earlier and seduce Ántonia.

Commentary

Because of the rift between Ántonia and Mrs. Harling, Jim no longer feels comfortable visiting the Harlings. After the Vannis leave town, he starts sneaking out at night to attend dances at the Firemen's Hall but is forced to give them up when Grandmother discovers his deceit. The happy days of Jim's childhood are clearly waning. When Ántonia goes to work for the Cutters, we feel that she too has taken a wrong path and may be heading for trouble.

The scene in which Ántonia scolds Jim for fervently kissing her reveals her realistic, down-to-earth qualities, which stand in opposition to Lena, who is more romantic, fragile, and dream-like. Later, Lena foolishly wears high-heeled slippers to the picnic in the country and lazily draws her fingers through Jim's hair to get the sand out; in contrast, Ántonia pushes Lena away, declaring "You'll never get it out like that," and gives his hair a rough tousling, finishing with "something like a box on the ear." Also implied here is that Ántonia is annoyed with Lena's seductive games and takes out her annoyance on Jim.

The picnic is significant because it's the last such outing that Jim and Ántonia will have together as young people. Cather treats it like a summary of the past, a recap of the present, and a prediction of the future. Jim and Ántonia talk about Mr. Shimerda, life in Bohemia, and their own arrivals in Nebraska. Jim has indeed become Mr. Shimerda's cultural heir—as the old man knew he would when he promised to give Jim his gun. He often thinks about Mr. Shimerda. He feels a sense of peace when he visits the lone grave on the corner of the Shimerda property, and he tells Ántonia that he had her father in mind when he wrote his moving graduation speech. When the other girls arrive, they too talk about their families and their own plans for the future.

Literary Device

The most famous image in this book, perhaps in all of Cather's writing, comes at the end of this chapter: the momentary silhouette of a pioneer's plow against the sun. This symbol can be interpreted in a number of ways. On a grand scale, the image can represent the pioneers, larger than life, conquering the land, then fading into obscurity when the frontier was settled. The plow and its fading in the twilight can also mean that our own accomplishments, which seem so great to us, are really only a small part of a greater whole; recall Chapter II of Part I, when Jim is sitting in the garden and imagining himself part of "something complete and great." On a more personal level, the plough against the sun represents Jim's and Ántonia's childhoods, which are drawing to a close and will never again be the driving force for them that it has been until now.

Glossary

a tall bonnet with bristling aigrettes   a lady's tall hat with bunches of the long, white, showy plumes of the egret used for ornament.

arnica   any of a number of plants of the composite family, bearing bright yellow flowers on long stalks with clusters of leaves at the base; here, a preparation made from certain of these plants, once used for treating sprains and bruises.

Cutter was one of the "fast set" of Black Hawk business men   Cather is suggesting that Wick Cutter came to the frontier because there were fewer laws governing behavior, allowing him to get away with things that could have landed him in jail on the East Coast.

dumb-bell   a device usually used in pairs, consisting of round weights joined by a short bar, by which it is lifted or swung about in the hand for muscular exercise.

elder   any of a genus of shrubs and small trees of the honeysuckle family, with compound leaves and flat-topped clusters of small white flowers followed by red or purple berries.

soft piles of chaff   piles of husks of wheat or other grain separated in threshing or winnowing.

enter the freshman class at the university without conditions   Jim does extra studying at home during his last year of high school so he won't have to take college preparatory courses in the fall.

poultice   a hot, soft, moist mass, as of flour, herbs, or mustard, sometimes spread on cloth, applied to a sore or inflamed part of the body.

spring wagon   a light wagon.

telling raw stories   telling bawdy stories.

Wilber   A small town in southeastern Nebraska, settled primarily by Bohemians.

Book III: Lena Lingard
Chapters I–IV

Summary

Jim studies diligently during his freshman year at college and stays in Lincoln through the following summer. Gaston Cleric, a Latin teacher, becomes his mentor. Cleric awakens Jim's love for the classics. Although he admires Cleric's scholarship, Jim knows that his own mind is too crowded by memories of people and places from his past for him ever to be a scholar, and this fact annoys him.

One evening, Lena Lingard appears at Jim's door, and he learns that she's been in Lincoln all winter. She owns a small dressmaking shop and has done well, but she's hesitated to visit Jim because she heard that he was very studious. They talk of home and of Ántonia, who has bragged that Jim will someday be richer than Mr. Harling. Ántonia has made up with the Harlings and now works for Mrs. Gardener at the hotel. Lena also says that Ántonia is engaged to marry Larry Donovan.

Shortly thereafter, Jim and Lena begin attending plays together. They are particularly moved by Dumas' *Camille*, and Jim is glad he didn't invite a college girl, who would talk during the intermission about shallow things like college dances. Lena seems quite mature.

Jim often takes Sunday breakfast with Lena, and he discovers that her southern landlord has a crush on her, as has the Polish violinist, Ordinsky, who lives across the hall. At first, Ordinsky thinks Jim's intentions toward Lena are dishonorable, but he decides later that Jim wants what's best for her. In love with Lena himself, Jim begins to neglect his studies.

Cleric writes Grandfather Burden, asking that Jim be allowed to accompany him to Harvard to finish college. Grandfather gives permission. Lena is a little hurt when Jim tells her the news, but she understands his reasons for leaving, and she doesn't try to stop him.

At the end of the term, Jim visits his grandparents in Black Hawk, returns to Virginia to visit relatives, then heads for Harvard. He is nineteen years old.

Commentary

Jim tries to study diligently at college, but he discovers that his mind is too full of memories of people and places from his past. He's frustrated at the amount of space Jake and Otto and Russian Peter take up in his mind. His obsession with nostalgia contrasts with Ántonia's way of living: She embraces her heritage and adjusts to whatever happens in life. Jim tries to shape his life; Ántonia lets life shape her. As a result, Ántonia is happier than Jim, who feels that his happiest days are over— "the best days are the first to flee."

Cather makes her characters often seem larger than life by presenting them through Jim's eyes and by linking them to the classics. For example, Jim compares the hired girls to the poetry of Virgil: "If there were no girls like them in the world," he says, "there would be no poetry." He also relates farm life to the classics when he recalls words from Virgil's *Georgics*, stating that "the pen was fitted to the matter as the plough is to the furrow."

Against the bleakness of the April prairie, Cather sets the glittering and tragic story of Camille. Jim compares himself and Lena to two jackrabbits running on the prairie; they are innocent and unsophisticated. The author adds a touch of irony when Jim and Lena walk home after the play under the umbrella that Mrs. Harling gave Jim as a graduation present. We know she wouldn't approve of his associating with Lena, just as Grandmother Burden wouldn't have approved of Lena using her name to gain entry to Jim's rooming house.

Lena is attractive to men because she is kind to all of them: the old ones, the lonely ones, the odd ones, and the young brash ones like Jim. Lena represents the delights of love—without ties or responsibilities. She is spring, youth, romance. Her colors are blue, white, and gold. She carries jonquils and hyacinths and has an aura of lilac and violet. Yet her easy-going, permissive way of giving love, and her idea of what marriage means, seem empty in contrast to the down-to-earth, solid qualities of Ántonia.

At the close of this section, Jim is nineteen, has had a youthful crush, and now seems destined to settle down to a respectable career.

Glossary

"Optima dies . . . prima fugit" A Latin phrase meaning "the best days are the first to flee." The quotation is from Virgil's *Georgics*, which opens with this statement: "In the lives of mortals, the best days are the first to flee."

noblesse oblige the inferred obligation of people of high rank or social position to behave nobly or kindly toward others.

Book IV: The Pioneer Woman's Story
Chapters I–IV

Summary

It takes Jim two years to finish his pre-law studies at Harvard. During a brief visit back to Black Hawk, he finds the town buzzing with gossip. Ántonia went to Denver with Larry Donovan, who jilted her, and she returned home unmarried and pregnant with his child. Now back on the farm, she has become Ambrosch's drudge.

Tiny Soderball went to Seattle and opened a hotel for sailors, which will be the ruin of her, the townspeople say; Jim gives us a glimpse into the future: Tiny will go to Alaska when gold is discovered and open a hotel; a dying Swedish prospector whom she cares for will deed her his claim, and she will become wealthy. Later, Tiny will persuade Lena to open a dressmaking shop in San Francisco.

When Jim stops in the photographer's shop to arrange sittings for his grandparents, he sees a photo of Ántonia's baby in a large gilt frame. He feels a compulsion to talk to his old friend. When he asks Mrs. Harling what happened to Ántonia, she suggests that he visit the Widow Steavens, who is closest to Ántonia and will know better than anyone else.

In early August, Jim visits the Widow Steavens, who tells him Ántonia's story. Larry Donovan wrote Ántonia that his railroad run had been changed and they would have to live in Denver. Ambrosch took her to the station and gave her $300, wages she'd earned while she had been hired out. In Denver, Ántonia cared for Donovan when he was ill, then he deserted her when her money was gone. She learned that he'd been fired and had not even tried to find another job. She returned to the Shimerda farm, where she bore her baby alone in her room. The Widow Steavens wishes Ántonia could marry and raise a family, but can see little hope for that now.

The next afternoon, Jim walks over to the Shimerda farm, where he sees Ántonia's baby. Later, he and Ántonia visit beside Mr. Shimerda's grave, feeling that it's the fittest place to talk to each other. He tells her that he plans to join a law firm owned by a relative of his mother's in New York City. Ántonia says she couldn't live in a city. "I like to be where I know every stack and tree, and where all the ground is friendly," she says. She tells him that even if he never comes back, he will always be with her in memory, and she will tell her daughter about all they did together. Her father, she says, has "been dead all these years, and yet he is more real to me than almost anybody else." As they part at twilight, Jim feels the earth pulling at him; he wishes he could be a little boy again and stay here. As he walks back to the Widow Steavens' farm, he feels that a little boy and girl are running beside him, "laughing and whispering to each other in the grass."

Commentary

The author contrasts both Tiny and Lena with Ántonia. Lena has made money, has never really loved anyone, and has never been hurt by a romantic attachment. Tiny has wanted only money and that is all she has found. At this point in the novel, Ántonia, a good soul with greater inner strength than either Lena or Tiny, has experienced nothing but grief, hard work, and her illegitimate baby. Cather describes the emptiness of Tiny's life: "She was like someone in whom the faculty of becoming interested is worn out." In contrast, "the faculty of becoming interested" is what constitutes much of Ántonia's strength.

Jim describes the changes that have taken place on the land since he went away: Wooden houses have replaced the old sod ones, and beside them are little orchards and big red barns. This progress pleases him; he feels as though he is "watching the growth of a great man or of a great idea." Here, Cather is making a correlation between Jim and the land; they have grown up together.

Ántonia exhibits her maternal qualities by not complaining about carrying Larry Donovan's baby, nor complaining when she gave birth. She continued to work on the farm until the baby was born and then, proud of her child, she allowed the baby's photo to be displayed in a fancy gilt frame at a photographer's shop.

The character of Larry Donovan is vividly drawn: He seems to be a man without any principles. In contrast, we glimpse Ambrosch's good side; we saw his concern for Mr. Shimerda's soul, when he gave $300 to Ántonia, helped her pack, and took her to the train. But, as he did after Mr. Shimerda was buried, he reverted back to his surly self again.

As Jim and Ántonia are saying good-bye, he seems to realize why he has always been attracted so strongly to her. She is tied to the land. No matter where he goes, she will always go with him, just as the land and his heritage will go with him. He tells her: "I'd have liked to have you for a sweetheart, or a wife, or my mother or my sister—anything that a woman can be to a man. The idea of you is a part of my mind; you influence my likes and dislikes, all my tastes, hundreds of times when I don't realize it. You really are a part of me."

Jim has gotten an education. He has the promise of a job, with the implication of great financial success. Yet from this excerpt in the final paragraph of this section—". . . I could almost believe that a boy and girl ran along beside me, as our shadows used to do, laughing and whispering to each other in the grass"—we are left with the impression that Jim doesn't really enjoy life anymore. We see that he is leaving his roots because that's what is expected of him. Consciously or unconsciously, he is following the path that the Black Hawk townspeople believe leads to success. Jim, like the other town boys, has become another cog in the machine of mediocrity and will never have the kind of personal success that even the hired girls will have.

Book V: Cuzak's Boys
Chapters I–III

Summary

Twenty years pass. Jim has had little contact with Ántonia. While traveling through Europe, he sent her pictures from Bohemia, and she wrote and thanked him, telling him the names and ages of her children. He heard from Tiny that Ántonia's husband "was not a man of much force, and she had had a hard life." Jim has been afraid to see Ántonia again because he wants to remember her as she was—he doesn't want to be disappointed. Finally, Lena persuades him to go see Ántonia.

When Jim arrives by open buggy at the Cuzak farm, Ántonia's husband and eldest son are away. At first Ántonia doesn't recognize Jim. He looks at her and sees that she is "battered but not diminished"; her identity is intact. Ántonia is delighted when she recognizes him, then becomes suddenly fearful, asking if someone has died. Jim reassures her that he didn't come for a funeral. She introduces him to her children, and then she and Jim walk in the orchard and talk about the days when they were young.

After supper, Leo and Yulka furnish music. Leo, who has inherited Mr. Shimerda's violin, plays the instrument very well for a self-taught boy. Yulka plays the organ, but not quite as well as Leo plays the violin. Ántonia brings out a box of photographs, and as they look at the photos, Jim senses a harmony among the members of the family. He finds that Ántonia's children know all about the people whom she and Jim grew up with.

At bedtime, Jim chooses to sleep in the haymow with two of the boys. He lies awake for a long time, thinking about how Ántonia turned out, how her fire did not diminish.

The next day, Ántonia's husband and son Rudolph return. Jim learns that long ago Cuzak came to Nebraska to visit his cousin, Anton Jelinek, and to consider settling here. He noticed Ántonia, realized that she was exactly the kind of girl he'd always hoped to meet, and they were married. Rudolph tells the story of how Wick Cutter killed his wife, then himself, making sure that he survived her long enough so that her family, whom he detested, wouldn't inherit his money.

Cuzak was born and raised in a Bohemian city, and at first he was very lonely on the plains. Because of Ántonia's strength, however, and because she was able to help in the fields, he stayed. He would like to visit the Old Country again, someday when the boys are old enough to take care of the farm themselves, but he has no regrets about putting down roots here.

Jim says good-bye to the Cuzak family and promises to go hunting with Ambrosch and Rudolph the following summer. His mind is full of trips he plans to take with the boys, and, even after they are grown up, he wants to "tramp along a few miles of lighted streets with Cuzak himself."

Jim takes the train to Black Hawk, and, walking down its streets, he realizes that most of his old friends have either died or moved away. He becomes bored and finally ends up wandering around a nearby pasture, where he stumbles upon the road that he and Ántonia followed when they arrived on the prairie thirty years ago. He remembers the feeling of isolation that he had that night. Now, as he once again walks along the familiar road, he has "the sense of coming home to myself, and of having found out what a little circle man's experience is." This road launched him and Ántonia on a journey, their paths parted, and now it has brought them together again. He feels at peace at last because "whatever we had missed, we possessed together the precious, the incommunicable past."

Commentary

One of Cather's main purposes in this section is to bring Jim and Ántonia together again and examine how time has changed each of them.

Literary Device

Jim finds Ántonia "battered but not diminished," and he realizes that she was—and still is—a symbol of life. Her happiness bursts out from the dark areas of her life just as the children rush upward—like an explosion of life—from the dark cave. The cave reminds us of the dugout where the Shimerdas lived when they first arrived in Nebraska; it symbolizes all the darkness and all the hardships of Ántonia's life, which she has made fruitful.

Literary Device

In the scene when Ántonia is displaying and showing the photographs, Cather contrasts her with Lena, who is essentially unchanged in appearance and who has lived a shallow, static life. Ántonia, on the other hand, bears scars from her hard life, but her life has been more fulfilling than Lena's. When thinking about Ántonia's lost teeth, Jim realizes that he knows "so many women who have kept all the things that she had lost, but whose inner glow has faded." Whatever else is gone, Ántonia has not lost the fire of life. She is a "rich mine of life like the founders of early races." Here again, Cather links her characters with the classical and mythological past. Ántonia is triumphant, larger than life, magnificent against the prairie—like the plow against the sun in Book II.

Cuzak and Jim are similar in that both left their roots to settle in unfamiliar lands. But Cuzak has put down new roots, mostly due to Ántonia's help; Jim often feels rootless. Even Jim's job—which requires extensive traveling—emphasizes that he is adrift. At the end of the novel, he finally admits to himself that he has come home, and he plans to spend many more years returning to Nebraska, spending time with Ántonia and her family. He realizes that he may have lost something by being away for twenty years, that both he and Ántonia may have lost something—although, as she has always done, Ántonia has adapted to the ever-flowing current of years. In the future, Jim plans to revisit Ántonia and her family and learn from their Old Country wisdom how to more fully appreciate people and life itself.

Glossary

breaking up this place and making the first crops grow Cuzak is referring to plowing his land and making it suitable for growing crops.

capote a long cloak, usually with a hood. Cather is metaphorically referring to the green feathers on the ducks' heads and necks as such a cloak.

he'll be rich some day Here, Ántonia equates hard work with financial success, as did most of the immigrant pioneers.

hollyhocks tall, usually biennial plants of the mallow family, with palmately lobed leaves, a hairy stem, and large, showy flowers of various colors in elongated spikes.

Jan   the Bohemian equivalent of *John*; pronounced "yahn."

Niobrara   a river flowing from eastern Wyoming east through northern Nebraska into the Missouri River.

kolaches   (ko-LAH-cheese) small, round Bohemian pastries with fruit filling in their centers. The Ceske Kolaces (Czech kolaches) that Ántonia and her family eat are made with lard and require much time to make (the dough must rise five separate times). Josie Macha Nemec shared this modern, and quite tasty, equivalent still made by the Czechs in southeast Nebraska.

Refrigerator Butter Kolaches

4 cups sifted all-purpose flour	1 cup cold milk
1 cup butter or margarine	3 egg yolks
2 tablespoons sugar	1 egg
2 packages yeast	2 teaspoons salt

Cut butter or margarine into flour as for pie crust. Mix together sugar, salt, and dry yeast; add flour mixture. Beat yolks, cold milk, and one egg together, and add to flour mixture. Stir together until elastic, adding more flour, if needed. Place in a bowl, cover, and refrigerate overnight. The next day, preheat oven to 400 degrees. Roll dough into a 1-inch thick sheet and cut into 2-inch circles. Place on ungreased sheets; let rise until almost double. Make depression in center of each circle with fingers and fill with your favorite filling. Let finish rising until double. Bake 15–20 minutes.

Prune Filling

Cook 50 prunes until soft. Drain, pit, and mash. Add 4 tablespoons sugar and a small amount of the prune juice you drained, if needed. Prune, poppy seed, apricot, and cottage cheese are traditional kolache fillings, but you may substitute almost any canned pie filling (cherry is particularly good).

CHARACTER ANALYSES

Ántonia Shimerda Cuzak

Ántonia has a resilient inner strength that drives her to succeed and helps her survive adversity. In this way, like the plow against the sun, she symbolizes the invincible pioneer spirit. From the time of her arrival on the prairie, she believes that a person who works hard will become wealthy. "Wealth," of course, can mean a lot of land and money, but, more important here, wealth is synonymous with whatever is rich in spirit and understanding.

On the train that brings Jim and Ántonia to Black Hawk, the conductor comments on the young girl's "pretty brown eyes." Later, when Jim first meets Ántonia at her family's dugout, again he is caught by her arresting, unusual eyes: "They were big and warm and full of light, like the sun shining on brown pools in the wood." From the very start, Cather is imbuing Ántonia with the qualities of warmth, generosity, and earthiness.

Jim has met Ántonia for only a matter of minutes, but she immediately reveals her generosity and impulsiveness by trying to give him her ring. Later, she reveals her enormous capacity for compassion by crying for the little green insect that she knows will not survive the winter. She further reveals her maternal nature when she grieves for Peter and Pavel and when she feels protective toward Jim. Even after Jim kills the snake, ostensibly making himself her protector, she looks out for him, warning him about Lena's possibly distracting him from his future plans. Ántonia makes excuses for her mother's greedy, accusatory behavior when the Burdens bring food, but she herself never complains. She looks for the good in life and doesn't dwell on the bad. She is ambitious for her family, even for the overbearing Ambrosch.

When Ántonia's father dies, she is crushed, but because she is a realist, she recovers quickly and takes his place in the fields, working beside Ambrosch and picking up masculine traits that disappoint Jim. Cather again associates Ántonia with the earth when she says, "Her neck came up strongly out of her shoulders, like the bole of a tree out of the turf." Ántonia's grasp on reality is reinforced when Jim accuses her of trying to be like Ambrosch and complains that she isn't "nice" all the time, as she used to be. "If I live here, like you," she tells him, "that is different. Things will be easy for you. But they will be hard for us."

After the Burdens move from the country into Black Hawk, Jim's grandmother persuades Mrs. Harling to hire Ántonia to work for them; she also convinces Ambrosch that such a move will benefit him because "any connection with Christian Harling would strengthen his credit." At the Harlings, Ántonia learns how chores are done in a well-ordered home. Because of the Harlings' many children, Ántonia learns how to be a good mother. She gets along well with Mrs. Harling because they both love life.

But Ántonia's spirit cannot be easily controlled. She is young, inexperienced, and likes to do things her own way. Although she believes that hard work is the path to success, she believes in indulging herself. This leads to her rift with her newfound family. When forced to choose between working for the Harlings and attending the dances, she chooses the dances and goes to work for the town's spiritually warped moneylender, Wick Cutter. Instinctively, Ántonia senses Cutter will try to seduce her, so she comes to Grandmother Burden for help. After Cutter assaults Jim in bed, thinking he is Ántonia, she goes to work as a housekeeper for the Gardeners, who own the hotel.

Ántonia begins dating Larry Donovan, a mere train conductor, but she talks of him as if he were "president of the railroad." She naively believes that he loves her, follows him to Denver, and cares for him when he's sick. Everyone else, however, particularly Jim, can see that he is leading her on. They are proven right when Ántonia's money runs out and Larry abandons her. Ántonia realizes that, despite the fact that she's pregnant, she must return to the farm.

Throughout her life, Ántonia does what must be done; as a realist, she accepts what happens as the natural course of things, and she accepts the consequences of her actions without complaint. When she goes into labor with Larry Donovan's child, she shuts herself in her room and gives birth without calling for help, without so much as a groan. Later, she is so proud of her baby that she allows the local photographer to display the baby's photo in a fancy frame in his shop.

In Book IV, when Jim meets Ántonia beside her father's grave, he realizes that adversity has caused her to increase in strength and understanding. Twenty years later, we see Ántonia as the mother of a large, loving family. The family members do not hesitate to touch one another nor to help one another. Ántonia's abundant potential for motherhood has come to fruition. "Battered but not diminished," she is the symbol of the earth, of all motherhood, the ideal for which all men search.

Jim Burden

Whereas Ántonia represents the pioneer who builds an abundant, promising future from a wasteland, Jim Burden represents the established settlers who have grown complacent, superior, and rigid in their thinking. To Ántonia, the road to success in life has many possible branches; to Jim and other Black Hawk citizens, there is only one acceptable road. Jim symbolizes the pioneer gone soft.

Jim's memories of Ántonia comprise the main body of the novel. He admires her and is drawn to her in such a way that his memories of her have been burned into his mind. In the opening chapter we see him as a 10-year-old orphan, arriving for the first time in Nebraska. Although the journey pleases and excites him, he sinks into a deep depression as the wagon carrying him to his grandparents' farm bumps along through the pitch-blackness. He feels erased from existence, blotted out. Cather is revealing his keen sensitivity and is suggesting that the slate has been wiped clean, that the future is his to create, that he has no limitations. This is also implied at the end of the opening Chapter I: " . . . here, I felt, what would be would be." In the next chapter, when Jim daydreams in Grandmother Burden's garden, he feels a part of something whole: " . . . that is happiness; to be dissolved into something complete and great."

While Jim grows up on the farm, we see him eagerly absorbing new experiences, but we also see some indications of his conventionality. For example, he is irritated with Ántonia for treating him like an inferior because she is older; he feels that he should be the dominant one—regardless of age—because he is a boy and she is a girl. After Ántonia's father's death, he disapproves of her working in the fields like a man, because it isn't feminine. Jim is upset when reality differs from his concept of the world. His attitude contrasts with Ántonia's acceptance of whatever happens as the natural course of events. Ántonia is a realist; Jim is too often a romantic idealist.

Jim's idealism is illustrated by his attitude toward the hired girls. He admires them and criticizes the townspeople for arrogantly looking down on them—that is, the girls are good enough for the boys of Black Hawk to have fun with, but they're not good enough to marry. Ironically, it won't be long before Jim will do precisely what he's condemning these boys for.

Still young, Jim is easily influenced by the judgments and opinions of others. He is thrilled when the hired girls admire his graduation speech, and he agrees—if reluctantly—to stay the night at Wick Cutter's house (in place of Ántonia). When his grandmother objects to his attending the dances at the Firemen's Hall, he stays away. Later, when Jim decides to marry, he doesn't choose a wife from the hired girls; he marries a woman with both money and class.

At college Jim learns a greater appreciation of the classics than he'd had at home, and he compares the people from his own childhood to people in the works of Virgil. He's introduced to a new world of music and opera, which he asks Lena Lingard to share. Their brief love affair causes him to neglect his schoolwork and this somewhat parallels Ántonia's affair with Larry Donovan, but the consequences are not so devastating for Jim as they are for Ántonia. When he realizes how time spent with Lena is affecting his work, he breaks off their affair and transfers to Harvard.

When Jim returns to Black Hawk, he sees a photograph of Ántonia's baby and longs to visit his old friend, but he initially finds it difficult to forgive her for throwing herself away on such a cheap fellow as Larry Donovan. Even now, he appears irresistibly drawn to Ántonia. Widow Steavens tells him the story of Ántonia's betrayal, and when he finally visits Ántonia, he can't deny that she is very important to him, yet he goes away and will not see her again for twenty years. He is afraid to return, afraid he will be disappointed.

After two decades, however, Jim's curiosity overcomes him, and he visits Ántonia and her family on their farm in Nebraska. Although Jim has prospered materially, he seems spiritually empty. This emptiness in Jim's life, twenty years later, is contrasted with the fullness of Ántonia's. Ántonia has not achieved great material wealth, but her spirit is free, full, and vital, and it is as optimistic as it was when they were children. He is glad that he has found her again, and he plans to spend more time with her and her family. Although his life has turned out as sterile as the lives of Lena and Tiny, he recognizes that through Ántonia's family, he can come home again.

Anton Cuzak

Anton Jelinek's cousin, Anton Cuzak, enters the novel in the last book. When Jim returns to Black Hawk and meets Ántonia's family, he also meets her husband, Anton Cuzak. Jim was aware she had married because she had signed an earlier letter to Jim "Ántonia Cuzak." Before meeting Anton, Jim is told about him from both Tiny and Lena. Tiny says Ántonia has not "done very well" and Cuzak is "not a man of much force" so Ántonia has had a hard life. But that picture is softened by Lena who says, "There's nothing the matter with Cuzak. You'd like him. He isn't a hustler, but a rough man would never have suited Tony." And so, Jim meets Ántonia's husband with these varying ideas in his mind.

His reaction to Anton is that he is a "crumpled little man" with a curly moustache, black hair, red lips, and a ruddy color. He is immediately drawn to Anton's good nature and humor. Also, Jim sees that Anton completes Ántonia: "she was the impulse and he the corrective." Anton's frankness, his good nature and his humorous philosophy draw Jim closer to Ántonia's family.

Cuzak's history goes back to parents and relatives who worked hard in the Old Country. Anton apprenticed with them and worked in a fur shop in Vienna. As a young man, he found the work good, the money plentiful, and life filled with lots of social events and very little financial savings. Eventually, he came to Nebraska by way of New York and Florida. Hearing that his cousin was in Nebraska, he visited Anton Jelinek and was smitten by Ántonia.

They married and had ten children, in addition to Martha, Ántonia's first child, fathered by Larry Donovan. This large family and their farm keep Anton and Ántonia anchored and down to earth. They now own the farm free and clear, but every so often Anton is offered good money for it and he thinks about leaving. Throughout these years Ántonia has talked him out of leaving, and they appear to complement each other. Even though, in the Old World, Anton was a "man of the city," who liked theatres, lighted streets, and music, he is now a part of Black Hawk, and Tony's warm heart has kept him here. Although Anton would like to visit Europe again, he is a quiet and companionable husband for Ántonia. Always he is drawn back to the farm, just like Jim Burden, by Ántonia's warm heart and loving spirit. Jim finds Anton a sociable and friendly man, a good companion for the future when he returns to visit his prairie roots.

Mr. Shimerda

Mr. Shimerda, Ántonia's father, is the most tragic character in Cather's story and his life is short-lived on the prairie. But his legacy lives on in his daughter Ántonia, her children, and in his influence on

Jim Burden. His earlier years in Europe reveal a sensitive, artistic, and respected man, but his life on the prairie, filled with loneliness and suffering, are too devastating for his delicate nature. When he dies, Ántonia is left without his parental support, but she manages to endure.

In the Old World of Bohemia, Mr. Shimerda was a weaver or tailor by trade and a violinist by avocation. Respected by all, he had wages and a reputation as a man of honor. The gun he gives to Jim was a present from a rich man in Bohemia who gave it to Mr. Shimerda as a gift for playing at his wedding. In the Old Country they were not beggars but by the time they came to America and made money changes and bought train tickets, there was little money left. Ill-suited for a life in the wilderness, Mr. Shimerda was harassed by his wife, who thought that the New World would offer land to their sons and husbands for their daughters. Her greed was what brought the gentle weaver to the Nebraska wilderness.

Once in Nebraska, Mr. Shimerda's sensitive nature is disheartened by the snow and cold and inhuman life in a cave. This is not what he had envisioned for his wife and children and, as the husband and father, he should be the provider. He often went to see the Russians because he was homesick for Eastern Europe and Pavel would talk with him because Mr. Shimerda was a wonderful and patient listener. When Pavel dies and Peter leaves, Mr. Shimerda is depressed by their departure and the advent of winter. He no longer makes music and he is sad, longing for the Old Country. He has a hard time adjusting to the isolation and brutality of life in the wilderness.

When Jim and Ántonia see him hunting, Jim describes Mr. Shimerda's state of mind reflected in his "walking slowly, dragging his feet along as if he had no purpose." It is obvious that Mr. Shimerda brightens up when he sees his Ántonia, but Jim remembers that his smile "was so full of sadness, of pity for things, that I never afterward forgot it." When Jim visits the family with his grandmother, he sees the weariness and pain, the life of dirt and darkness, at the Shimerda cave. He imagines that "in the crowded clutter of their cave, the old man had come to believe that peace and order had vanished from the earth, or existed only in the old world he had left so far behind." How can he watch his family live like this? How can he provide for them?

The last time Jim sees Mr. Shimerda, the old man comes to Jim's grandparents' house at Christmas-time. The contrast between Jim's home and the Shimerda home must have been devastating for the old man. Here at Jim's grandparents' are warmth, light, happiness, and homemade presents. The old man's face changes from weariness to pleasure, and, stretched out before their fire, he remembers the Old Country and how life used to be.

Later, when Mr. Shimerda kills himself it is the depth of winter, and despair is all he sees. His suicide leaves Ántonia without a father and a spiritual support, because she was closest to him and she understood him with her heart. Often, Ántonia and Jim speak of Mr. Shimerda, and later they meet near his grave. Jim finds a peacefulness there that he cannot find in his adult life. He always felt Mr. Shimerda could see his future with "deep-seeing eyes," and the gentle man left Jim his prized possession: the gun from Bohemia. Jim is the keeper of Mr. Shimerda's memory, and he shares that with Ántonia. He often thinks of Mr. Shimerda and feels such a sense of peace that he makes Ántonia's father the subject of his graduation speech. He also comforts Ántonia by picturing her father's spirit heading back to his beloved Bohemia. Little Leo, Mr. Shimerda's grandson, is the legacy to the future, a child who lives on a free and clear farm and plays his grandfather's violin reluctantly.

In Mr. Shimerda's story is the human suffering, sacrifice, and endless struggle that marked the immigrant experience in the early days of the prairie. He would not live to see the next wave of immigrant girls who hired out, sent money home to their parents, and enabled them to buy the land for which they made such sacrifices. But his memory would live on in Ántonia and in the stories she tells her children about their grandfather.

Mrs. Shimerda

In many ways the opposite of her husband, Mrs. Shimerda is meanspirited, small-minded, shrewish, and grasping. She is never satisfied, always expecting more. Jim mentions that she always looks accusingly at those who have more than she does. It was her greed and desire for better things that brought the family to America. She saw the New World as an opportunity for her sons to own land and her daughters to marry well. Little did she realize that life on the Nebraska prairie would be isolated, brutal, and full of suffering. One can only imagine what she must have said to Mr. Shimerda for providing as poorly as he did once they were in Nebraska.

Her actions and words in the presence of the Burdens make her character quite clear. She is a terrible housekeeper, poor cook, and disagreeable in everything. Grandmother mentions that she could have used some of her neighbor's hens to start a henhouse but could not even manage to do that to help the family. Mrs. Shimerda disagrees over the cow the Burdens loan them, is unhappy over Ántonia's English lessons, and is envious and complaining that Jim's grandparents don't "give their share."

On visiting the Burden house, Mrs. Shimerda further shows her lack of class by complaining, making her jealousy clear, and whining that her lot in life is much worse than the Burdens, who have lived on the land and farmed it for many years already. Hard work does not seem to be the road to success for Mrs. Shimerda. Jim mentions that she might share things, but she always expected "substantial presents in return." Her visits are often dramatic and filled with greed and expectations. It is plain to see that Mrs. Shimerda's character is quite a contrast to that of her husband.

Although Jim is disgusted with Mrs. Shimerda and her actions and words, Grandmother tries to be charitable, giving her a cooking pot, sending food and presents on many occasions, and offering words of solace. She even says that her actions can be excused because she is a stranger in the country and is trying to provide for her family. But Jim presents a truer picture in his assessment that "she was a conceited, boastful old thing and even misfortune could not humble her." One can only hope that in the afterlife her husband was spared her complaints.

Lena Lingard and Tiny Soderball

Both of them immigrants and hired girls, Lena and Tiny are examples of early immigrants who go out into the world and are successful. Lena learns to be a dressmaker and later moves to San Francisco and has a thriving dress shop. On the other hand, Tiny leaves Black Hawk and starts a hotel in Seattle, later moving to the Klondike and becoming a wealthy woman. Both come into Jim's life, although Lena is definitely the one who influences him the most.

Lena is the sensuous Norwegian hired girl who, like Circe in Homer's *Odyssey*, distracts men and leaves them dreaming of pleasure. When Jim first meets her she has moved off the farm to Black Hawk and is learning dressmaking from Mrs. Thomas. Her reputation has preceded her: flirtatious and beautiful, she has driven Ole Benson to distraction so that his mentally deranged wife has come after Lena to kill her. Moving into Black Hawk, Lena becomes one of the hired girls who attends the dances and is quite popular with the men of the town. But she has no intention of marrying; she is satisfied to have a good time, make money, and never give her heart away.

In many ways, Lena is a foil for Ántonia. While Ántonia wants a home and family, Lena does not. Fastidious about her appearance, Lena is very fashionable and concerned about her looks, while Ántonia works in the fields and worries little about her clothes and appearance. While Ántonia is brought up strictly and loves to dance for the sake of having a good time and enjoying life, Lena is a woman of loose morals. Ántonia not only warns Mrs. Harling of this, but she also gets angry with Jim for spending so much time with Lena.

Before he leaves for the university, Jim spends a day having a picnic with many of his friends, but particularly Lena and Ántonia. During a conversation where Lena kisses Jim, Ántonia ends up scolding him because she sees he has a future and he does not want to tie himself down with a woman of Lena's caliber in Black Hawk. She, like her father, sees greater things for Jim. But Lena is quite a temptation. This influence is seen even more when she moves to Lincoln, where Jim is living, and once again begins a relationship with him.

They attend plays together and have breakfast together; soon it is obvious to Jim that many men, including Lena's landlord, are a little in love with her. The more Jim sees Lena, the more he has sensuous dreams of her and falls in love with her, but his heart keeps wishing the dreams were of Ántonia. Lena's role in Jim's life is to represent the delights of love without the responsibility. She is a beautiful, sensuous, and distracting woman who eventually causes Jim to have trouble with his studies. In fact, his mentor, Gaston Cleric, recognizes Jim's preoccupation and suggests eventually that Jim accompany him when he leaves for the East.

Lena's character is softened by the scene where she helps her brother buy a handkerchief for their mother. She misses her family after she moves to Black Hawk, and it is very apparent that Lena is devoted to her mother, sending her money and thinking about future help she can give her. Lena seems to be a warmhearted and doting daughter. As time goes by, she makes a great deal of money and does not attach herself lovingly to any man. As such, she is a contrast to Ántonia, a distraction to Jim, and an example of an immigrant girl who leaves the farm, hires out, and helps the family better itself.

Tiny Soderball is also a hired girl who moves to Black Hawk, hires out, and attends the dances and picnics. Like Lena, she enjoys life and dates many of the local boys but, because she is a hired girl, the young men of the town cannot offer her a future. They must marry within their own set. So she, like Lena, leaves town after working for Mrs. Gardener at the hotel. Although the townspeople criticize her for opening a hotel in Seattle, she does well there and moves on to the Klondike during the Gold Rush. There she also opens a hotel for miners and inherits a claim from a Swede who made a fortune. Unlike Lena, eventually the thrill of conquest fades for Tiny, and she becomes cynical about life. Like Lena, she is an example of the immigrant daughters who hired out, learned a trade, helped their family, and did well.

CRITICAL
ESSAYS

The Real Ántonia

When the Cather family left their country farm and moved into the small town of Red Cloud, Nebraska, in 1884, Mary Miner, the second Miner daughter, brought Willa a bottle of perfume, nestled in a red plush slipper. Thus began Cather's lifetime friendship with the Miner family, who were to become the models for the Harlings in *My Ántonia*.

Cather's friendship with Annie Sadilek, the model for Ántonia, blossomed when Annie was employed as the Miner family's "hired girl." It's possible, however, that the girls may have known each other earlier, when they both lived in the country. The road to Red Cloud passed near the Sadilek dugout, and one of Willa's favorite pastimes was visiting her immigrant neighbors. In fact, Cather has said that she "saw a good deal of [the original Ántonia] from the time I was eight until I was twelve."

The Sadileks left their village of Mzizovic, Bohemia, in October 1880. There was only one other Bohemian family on their ship, the rest were Polish, and they landed in America on November 5. Francis Sadilek had received letters from America that told of the country's beauty and prosperity, and he wanted his family to have a better life. What he ended up with was a 160-acre Nebraska farm with nothing on it but a sod house, a bed, and a four-lid stove.

The hard living conditions on the prairie, the dugouts, and the roads that were no more than a set of wagon tracks disillusioned Francis Sadilek. On February 15, he told his wife that he was going rabbit hunting. He took the shotgun he'd brought from the Old Country and went out. When he hadn't returned by 5:00 p.m., Mrs. Sadilek, Annie's older brother, and the man whom the Sadileks lived with went to search for him. They found him half-sitting in an old barn; he had shot himself in the head. He was buried on a corner of the Sadilek farm, at the crossroads, although his son Anton later moved the body to the Catholic section of the Red Cloud cemetery. Mrs. Sadilek and the two Sadilek boys are also buried there.

In a 1955 letter to a schoolgirl, Annie Sadilek Pavelka writes: " . . . most all is true that you read in the Book thoug [sic] most of the names are changed."

Willa Cather told the story of Francis Sadilek's suicide in her first published story, "Peter," written during her freshman year in college, and again in *My Ántonia*. In a 1934 letter to Carrie Miner Sherwood, she said that if she'd written only one thing in her life, it would have been *My Ántonia* because of the many times she'd heard about the Sadilek suicide story shortly after her family arrived in Nebraska.

Willa and Carrie speculated endlessly on Mr. Sadilek's occupation before he came to America and about why he'd taken his life. They also discussed the other Sadilek family members: the crippled little sister who didn't go to school, the deaf brother who tried to be friendly but usually startled people instead, the controlling older brother, and the demanding mother who wanted her family to be successful. Annie's mother always insisted that visitors take sugar with their coffee because she believed that being able to provide sugar was a sign of prosperity.

After her mother's death, Christina Sadilek, Annie's crippled younger sister, entered the St. Francis Convent at Lafayette, Indiana; convent records show the date as September 4, 1897. At the convent, Christina proved to be an excellent baker and was also given the duty of teaching young girls. This life apparently agreed with her because she lost all traces of the illness from which she'd suffered as a child.

Like Ántonia, Annie took over her father's chores after his death, but the work eventually proved to be too difficult, and she was finally forced to become a hired girl in the Miner home. She was a hard worker. Although she'd never cooked before, she soon learned how to prepare meals and how to sew. When Mrs. Miner gave her permission to use the sewing machine, she made all the clothes, including husking gloves, for her family. She made everyday shoes for herself out of cardboard, oil-cloth, and denim, which she tied to her feet with black tape. The shoes flapped when she hurried about breathlessly getting her work done.

Annie often went with the Miner children to the Red Cloud Opera House. She loved to dance and would have danced all night if she didn't have to get some sleep so she could work the next day. Because Annie was under eighteen, her family collected her wages, but Carrie Miner, the model for Frances Harling in *My Ántonia*, finally made sure that Annie had enough money left over for shoes.

Annie later went West to marry a brakeman for the Burlington railroad. After only a few weeks, however, he deserted her, and she returned to her family on the farm.

Cather went on to the university in Lincoln and soon began a promising journalism career. She moved away from Nebraska and lost touch with Annie, but, in 1914, she found her again. Although Edith Lewis suggests that this meeting took place in 1916, critic James Woodress points out that in 1914, while she was writing *The Song of the Lark*, Cather spent two weeks visiting immigrant friends in the Red Cloud area. Therefore, he maintains, it seems likely that she renewed her friendship with Annie at this time. Also, if we assume that *My Ántonia* begins in the year the Cathers arrived in Nebraska, then Jim Burden's return from New York to visit Ántonia would be in 1914.

Cather discovered that Annie had married a fellow Bohemian, John Pavelka, who would become the model for Neighbor Rosicky, in the short story of the same name. Moreover, Annie was mother to a clan of strong, healthy children. Her daughters were beautiful and her sons excelled in high school sports. Cather enjoyed her visits with the Pavelkas. She especially liked sitting at the long table in Annie's cheerful kitchen and she had long enjoyed Bohemian cooking—especially kolaches and Annie's banana cream pie. The food storage cave, characteristic of all Midwestern farm homes, described in the final section of the novel is an accurate depiction of the Pavelkas' food storage cave.

Cather got along well with Annie's sons, whose manners, she said, "would do credit to the family of a Grand Duke," and, when it was time for her to leave, they escorted her to her carriage. John Pavelka was as proud of his children as Annie was, agreeing that raising healthy and happy children was more important than acquiring land or money. John was fond of telling strangers that he was "the husband of *My Ántonia*," and one of the Pavelka sons, even as an old man, would proudly say, "I'm Leo, the mischievous one."

After her mother died in 1931, Cather returned to Red Cloud for a short while to visit old friends and tie up family affairs. Although she would continue writing letters and sending gifts to people she knew, including Annie Pavelka, she never went home again.

Annie died at the age of eighty-six on April 24, 1955, eight years to the day after Willa Cather's death, and is buried in the Cloverton Cemetery near Bladen, Nebraska. She became hard of hearing toward the end of her life, but she never lost the vitality or the energy that Willa Cather captured in Ántonia Shimerda. One of Annie's sons has said that his mother "was happier with a crust of bread and a new baby than someone else would be with a million dollars."

My Ántonia and Autobiography

Of all of Willa Cather's works, *My Ántonia* seems to contain the most elements drawn from the author's life—with the possible exception of "Old Mrs. Harris." Cather is thinly disguised as Jim Burden; many of Jim's thoughts and feelings in the novel were Cather's own thoughts and feelings while growing up. In the introduction, Cather's description of Jim could easily be a description of herself. Like Jim, Cather enjoyed visiting with immigrant neighbors; like Jim, she had a love for the classics and for drama; and, like Jim, when he was middle-aged, she revisited "Ántonia" (Anna Sadilek Pavelka, her model for Ántonia) and renewed their friendship. This reunion inspired Cather to begin writing *My Ántonia*.

Cather's first three novels, after the immature *Alexander's Bridge*, can be viewed as paralleling Cather's development as an artist and as a person. In *O Pioneers!* (written on the advice of Sarah Orne Jewett, who suggested to Cather that she write about things that were important to her), the land is of primary importance. In *Song of the Lark*, written while *O Pioneers!* was proclaiming Cather's arrival as a significant new writer, the development of Thea's art is important. In *My Ántonia*, these two worlds—land and art—are united, suggesting that this novel may be one reason why Cather wrote herself so thoroughly into the novel: she is reliving her own life to that point.

Cather's characters are usually composites of people she knew. In *My Ántonia*, many of them bear striking resemblances to friends and neighbors. The Miner Family, the Cather family's nearest neighbors, became the Harlings; Mrs. Holland, the hotel keeper, became Mrs. Gardener; two musicians, Blind Boone and Blind Tom, became Blind d'Arnault; Herbert Bates, one of Cather's university teachers, became Gaston Cleric.

Ántonia is one of two major characters in Willa Cather's works who are closely drawn portraits of real people; the other is Mrs. Forester in *A Lost Lady*, who was closely modeled after a former Nebraska governor's wife, Mrs. Garber. Annie was a hired girl to the Miner family and was a trustworthy, hard-working girl, well-liked by the townspeople—but none of them, including the family for whom she worked, sensed anything special about her. Cather did, however. She grew up with Annie, just as Jim Burden grows up with Ántonia in the novel.

Cather has said that most of her knowledge about Annie Pavelka came from the impressions of young men who knew her; most of our impressions of Ántonia come from Jim Burden.

Three years after the publication of *My Ántonia*, Cather stated that Annie was "one of the truest artists I ever knew in the keenness and sensitiveness of her enjoyment, in her love of people and in her willingness to take pains." This statement also describes Cather's portrait of Ántonia.

Mr. Shimerda's suicide is based on the suicide of Francis Sadilek, Annie's father. Like Mr. Shimerda, Mr. Sadilek loved music. Like Mr. Shimerda, he grew depressed about his bleak Nebraska existence. And, like Mr. Shimerda, he shot himself in the barn. *My Ántonia* was not the first work in which Cather told this story; she told it as early as 1892 in "Peter," her first published story.

In late 1915 and early 1916, Cather, who so disliked change, received a double blow from which she never fully recovered. In November, Judge McClung died, signaling the breakup of Murray Hill House, which was put up for sale. Cather and Isabelle spent a final Christmas there, and, shortly afterward, Isabelle told her friend she planned to marry concert violinist Jan Hambourg. Cather was heartbroken, worrying that the newlyweds would move to Europe, thus ending her friendship with Isabelle.

Not only did Cather dislike change in her personal life, but she resisted change in society. She was concerned that the past could be lost by the advance of progress. This intermingling of old and new is woven throughout *My Ántonia*. The famous plough against the sun is commonly interpreted as a symbol of the last pioneers.

Jim makes a picture book for Yulka as a Christmas present, using colored pictures from cards he brought with him from Virginia. When Ántonia asks Jim to join her on what will be their final picnic as children, she says: "Couldn't you happen along, Jim? It would be like old times." On his visit home before beginning law school at Harvard, Jim compares the built-up, tamed prairie with its vast wildness when he was young.

My Ántonia, then, was written at a critical time in Willa Cather's life. She was in her mid-forties, had seen many changes—not all of which she felt were for the better—and had just suffered two major shocks: the death of Judge McClung and the marriage of his daughter. The time seemed right for her life and her art to meet.

The Two Introductions

Willa Cather constructed *My Ántonia* from memories about people and places that were very dear to her and wove them together to form a larger story. For this reason, the body of the novel came easily for her. The introduction, however, was difficult to write, and she was never satisfied with it.

In the original introduction, written for the 1918 edition, the female narrator (possibly Cather herself) and Jim Burden meet on a train west of Chicago. He's a lawyer for a major railroad company, and she is a writer. The narrator dislikes Jim's wife and tells the reader why at great length. Despite his failed marriage, however, Jim has retained his romantic disposition and his love for the West, and he remains as impressionable as she remembers he was when they were children.

The narrator and Jim reminisce about growing up together on the Nebraska prairie, and their talk keeps returning to Ántonia, who "seemed to mean to us the country, the conditions, the whole adventure of our childhood." The narrator believes that Jim can tell Ántonia's story better than she: ". . . he had had opportunities that I, as a little girl who watched her come and go, had not." They both agree to record their memories of Ántonia.

The following winter, Jim arrives at the narrator's door with a completed manuscript, but he finds that his friend has jotted down only a few notes. Jim is surprised at the mention of notes. "I didn't arrange or rearrange," he says. "I simply wrote down what of herself and myself and other people Ántonia's name recalls to me. I suppose it hasn't any form. It hasn't any title, either." He writes "Ántonia" across the face of the manuscript, considers a moment, and then affixes "My" in front of the name. The narrator says that she is presenting us with Jim's manuscript, just as he gave it to her.

When *My Ántonia* was reissued in 1926, Cather eagerly took the opportunity to revise her introduction, making three changes of primary importance. First, the female narrator is gone; Cather (or someone very much like her) is not writing the introduction. Second, Jim is not inspired to write because of his conversation with the narrator, but has been at work on the manuscript long before he meets the narrator on the train. And third, the page devoted to Jim's wife, Mrs. Burden, has been reduced to less than a paragraph.

All of these changes strengthen not only the introduction, but also the novel. Because Jim decides to write the manuscript on his own, we know that he's been profoundly affected by his relationship with Ántonia. The long satirical description of Mrs. Burden in the original introduction unintentionally implies that Jim's judgment about women is not sound. If he misjudged his wife's character, why should we believe that his impressions of Ántonia are any more accurate?

This second introduction is an improved version of the first, retaining and strengthening its most important point: *My Ántonia* was written by a nonprofessional writer who had left his roots, was frustrated in life, and fondly and nostalgically remembering his youth in Nebraska as the happiest time of his life, recalling Cather's inscription at the beginning of the book: "The best days . . . flee first."

Willa Cather's Art

Decades before the term *throwaway society* came into vogue, Willa Cather was concerned that progress and technology were eroding society's appreciation of art. In a speech at Bowdoin College in Brunswick, Maine, on May 13, 1925, she warned:

> The novel has resolved into a human convenience to be bought and thrown away at the end of a journey. The cinema has had an almost devastating effect on the theater. Playwriting goes on about as well as usual, but the cheap and easy substitutes for art are the enemies of art.

She went on to relate a story of how she had tried to find Longfellow's *Golden Legend* at a bookstore in Portland that day. The bookstore didn't have it, and the manager told her he wouldn't sell it even if he had it. "He said he was cutting out all his two dollar books," Cather told her audience, "because people wanted Zane Grey and such."

One of Cather's complaints was that people who knew they had no talent for painting or music believed that they could sit down and write a novel, a good novel—if they chose to take the time. In other words, most people think that it doesn't take talent to write a novel.

A true artist, Cather says, should stretch the limits of his or her creativity, in order to strive for something new, rather than something that has been done many times before. In her essay, "On the Art of Fiction," Cather writes:

Writing ought either to be the manufacture of stories for which there is a market demand—a business as safe and commendable as making soap or breakfast foods—or it should be an art, which is always a search for something for which there is no market demand, something new and untried, where the values are intrinsic and have nothing to do with standardized values.

Cather believed that no book fewer than a hundred years old should be called a classic. Contemporary novels, she felt, should not be taught in schools. They should be discovered by students reading on their own. She believed that no teacher could discourage students from falling in love with silly books, but students who stumbled across good ones would treasure them far more than if a teacher assigned them.

When Cather first started writing novels, it took her several years and four books to settle on a style that suited her. *Song of the Lark*, for instance, was a stylistic departure from *O Pioneers!*. Whereas reviewers lauded *O Pioneers!* for its simple, straightforward style, they found *Song of the Lark* wallowing in detail. Her London publisher, William Heinemann, rejected it because of its complexity. Heinemann personally admired the book, but felt that Cather "had taken the wrong road, and that the full-blooded method, which told everything about everybody, was not natural to [her] and was not the one in which [she] would ever take satisfaction."

In her essay "My First Novels," she writes about returning to her earlier, simpler style with her next book, *My Ántonia*:

> Too much detail is apt, like any other form of extravagance, to become slightly vulgar; and it quite destroys in a book a very satisfying element analogous to what painters call "composition."

Unlike many writers, Cather did not become attached to her prose. She revised her work carefully, but once it was set in galleys, she would rarely make artistic changes. This was fortunate because after a book is set in type, it is costly for the publisher to change it, and most publishers charge authors for making other than critically necessary corrections. Occasionally, however, the muse would strike, and Cather, rethinking her story, was unable to control her urge to rewrite. This happened when she read through the proofs of *My Ántonia*, which resulted in the publisher billing her for nearly $150 for proof corrections.

Rose C. Field, in an article for the *New York Times Book Review*, December 21, 1924, asked Cather if *My Ántonia* was a good book because it was a story of the soil. Cather denied that the novel had anything to do with the country, or the city, or that it had a formula. She declared that it was "a story of people I knew. I expressed a mood, the core of which was like a folk-song. . . . The thing worthwhile is always unplanned. Any art that is a result of preconcerted plans is a dead baby."

CliffsNotes Review

Use this CliffsNotes Review to test your understanding of the original text, and reinforce what you've learned in this book. After you work through the review and essay questions, identify the quote section, and the fun and useful practice projects, you're well on your way to understanding a comprehensive and meaningful interpretation of *My Ántonia*.

Q&A

1. Jim Burden went to live with his grandparents on the Nebraska prairie because:

   a. his parents died.

   b. his father and mother went to Europe.

   c. his grandparents needed his help.

   d. he had too many brothers and sisters and his parents could not support them all.

2. As a child, Antonia faced many difficulties. Which of the following was **not** one of them?

   a. her father's death by suicide.

   b. a lack of warm clothing for the cold weather.

   c. a lack of food.

   d. her mother's deserting of the family.

3. Wick Cutter is:

   a. a designer of ladies' clothes.

   b. a moneylender.

   c. Jim's tutor at the university.

   d. a miner who struck it rich.

4. The story of Pavel and Peter illustrates all of the following *except*:

   a. the harshness of life on the prairie.

   b. the fears and difficulties of life in the Old World of Russia.

   c. the difficulty of sending for relatives in Europe.

   d. how Americans sometimes took advantage of immigrants financially.

5. In the end, Jim Burden underlines one of the many themes of the novel when he realizes:

a. he always loved Ántonia and should have married her.

b. the prairie is a source of peace and contentment for him.

c. his early life on the prairie did not prepare him for his Eastern education.

d. life in the East is much more fulfilling than the difficult life on the prairie.

Answers: (1) a. (2) d. (3) b. (4) c. (5) b.

Identify the Quote

In each of the following passages, Jim Burden describes one of the novel's characters. Identify whom Jim Burden is describing.

1. "[He] said little. When he first came in he kissed me and spoke kindly to me, but he was not demonstrative. I felt at once his deliberateness and personal dignity, and was a little in awe of him. The thing one immediately noticed about him was his beautiful, crinkly, snow-white beard."

2. "[H]e turned to me with his far-away look that always made me feel as if I were down at the bottom of a well. . . . [His smile], as he listened, was so full of sadness, of pity for things, that I never afterward forgot it."

3. "It was the first time [she] had been to our house, and she ran about examining our carpets and curtains and furniture, all the while commenting upon them . . . in an envious, complaining tone."

4. "[She] moved without exertion, rather indolently, and her hand often accented the rhythm softly on her partner's shoulder. . . . To dance 'Home, Sweet Home,' with [her] was like coming in with the tide."

5. "He was shorter than his older sons; a crumpled little man, with run-over boot-heels, and he carried one shoulder higher than the other. But he moved very quickly, and there was an air of jaunty liveliness about him."

6. "She was a battered woman now, not a lively girl; but she still had that something which fires the imagination, could still stop one's breath for a moment by a look or gesture that somehow revealed the meaning in common things. . . . All the strong things of her heart came out in her body, that had been so tireless in serving generous emotions. . . . She was a rich mine of life, like the founders of early races."

Answers: (1) Grandfather Burden. (2) Mr. Shimerda. (3) Mrs. Shimerda. (4) Lena Lingard. (5) Anton Cuzak. (6) Ántonia.

Essay Questions

1. Why does Willa Cather introduce Jim Burden and let him tell the story of Ántonia?

2. Explain how Cather adds depth and color to her novel by bringing in Old World roots (such as Pavel's wedding party story and Old Hata).

3. What incidents show that Ántonia is a maternal character?

4. Compare and contrast Ántonia with her parents. What character traits does she get from each?

5. What is the significance to the novel of the wedding party story that Pavel tells Mr. Shimerda?

6. Discuss the role of one of these characters (or groups of characters) in the novel: Lena Lingard, Otto Fuchs and Jake Marpole, Pavel and Peter, Wick Cutter, Mrs. Harling, or Anton Cuzak.

7. Trace the role of the seasons throughout the story and explain how nature has a symbolic purpose as well as an organizing purpose in the novel.

8. What techniques does Cather use to achieve unity in her novel?

9. Jim changes considerably through the course of the novel. What is he like at the beginning and how has he changed by the end? Explain the influences that have changed him.

10. Ántonia has also changed considerably. What is she like at the beginning of the novel and how has she changed by the end? Explain the influences that have changed her.

11. Give several examples of how Cather intermingles the past with the present to create a nostalgic effect or sense of loss.

12. If Ántonia had told this story, how would it have been different in several key respects?

13. The setting—life on the prairie in the late 1800s—affects Jim and Ántonia for the rest of their lives. How has this setting influenced their destinies?

14. There is a strong suggestion that social class plays a role in the settling of the prairie. How does Cather demonstrate this in her novel?

Practice Projects

1. Research Bohemia and use your information to explain what Ántonia's family life might have been like if her family had stayed in the Old Country.

2. Research the immigrant experience in America. Was the Shimerda experience typical of what many families expected and experienced in coming to America?

3. In what ways did Cather's life influence her novel? Pair up with another person and present an interview with the author to answer this question.

4. Create a journal, written by Ántonia, that portrays her thoughts about several key scenes/stories in the novel.

5. Pretend you are a researcher going back to Black Hawk in the late 1900s. Make up the story of what happened to Jim Burden, Ántonia and Anton, and their children after the story ended.

6. Create a collage that represents the prairie and the seasons that influenced the novel.

7. Create a set of letters that Jim and his grandmother might have exchanged during the years he was in the East going to school.

8. Read Cather's short story about another immigrant family, "Neighbor Rosicky," and compare and contrast it with *My Ántonia*.

CliffsNotes Resource Center

The learning doesn't need to stop here. CliffsNotes Resource Center shows you the best of the best—links to the best information in print and online about the author and/or related works. And don't think that this is all we've prepared for you; we've put all kinds of pertinent information at www.cliffsnotes.com. Look for all the terrific resources at your favorite bookstore or local library and on the Internet. When you're online, make your first stop www.cliffsnotes.com where you'll find more incredibly useful information about *My Ántonia*.

Books

This CliffsNotes book provides a meaningful interpretation of *My Ántonia* published by IDG Books Worldwide, Inc. If you are looking for information about the author and/or related works, check out these other publications:

Approaches to Teaching Cather's My Antonia, edited by Susan J. Rosowski, discusses materials and contains 23 scholar-teacher essays. New York: Modern Language Association of America, 1989.

The Landscape and the Looking Glass: Willa Cather's Search for Value, by John H. Randall III, contains multiple chapters on the themes and style of *My Ántonia* and discusses Cather's other works as well. Westport, Connecticut: Greenwood Press, 1973.

My Ántonia: The Road Home, by John J. Murphy, analyzes the history, content, importance of, and critical reception of the novel. Boston: Twayne Publishers, 1989.

The Voyage Perilous: Willa Cather's Romanticism, by Susan J. Rosowski, analyzes the effect of American materialism on Cather's themes. Lincoln, Nebraska: University of Nebraska Press, 1986.

Willa Cather: A Critical Biography, by E.K. Brown, describes Cather's life from Virginia to Nebraska, as well as her career and novels. Lincoln, Nebraska: University of Nebraska Press, 1987.

Willa Cather: Double Lives, by Hermione Lee, looks at Cather's work through a series of contradictions. New York: Vintage Books, 1991.

Willa Cather: The Emerging Voice, by Sharon O'Brien, describes—with a feminist viewpoint—Cather's writing and her life as both artist and woman. Cambridge, Massachusetts: Harvard University Press, 1997.

Willa Cather: A Literary Life, by James Woodress, offers a definitive biography of Cather, including her speeches, letters, interviews, and criticism. Lincoln, Nebraska: University of Nebraska Press, 1987.

Willa Cather: Writing at the Frontier, by Jamie Ambrose, is a sympathetic and accurate biography of Cather's life and fiction. New York: Berg Publishers, Ltd., 1988.

It's easy to find books published by IDG Books Worldwide, Inc. You'll find them in your favorite bookstores (on the Internet and at a store near you). We also have three Web sites that you can use to read about all the books we publish:

■   www.cliffsnotes.com

■   www.dummies.com

■   www.idgbooks.com

Internet

Check out these Web resources for more information about Willa Cather and *My Ántonia*:

Harvard University Willa Cather Site, www.courses.fas.harvard.edu/~cather/ — contains events celebrating Willa Cather, publications by and about her, a long bibliography, photographs, Cather quotations, and a biography.

Willa Cather, www.kutztown.edu/faculty/reagan/cather.html — contains a biography, a list of Cather's writings, criticisms, awards and honors, and a bibliography.

Willa Cather Pioneer Memorial and Educational Foundation Web Site, www.willacather.org/index.htm — an extensive site with photographs of places from Cather's life, an online store featuring related products, information on conferences on Cather, and information about the Pioneer Memorial and Educational Foundation.

Next time you're on the Internet, don't forget to drop by www.cliffsnotes.com. We created an online Resource Center that you can use today, tomorrow, and beyond.

Films and Other Recordings

The following films may be of use when studying Willa Cather and *My Ántonia*:

My Ántonia. Perf. Jason Robards, Eva Marie Saint, Neil Patrick Harris, Elina Löwensohn. 1995. A made-for-TV movie based on the novel by Willa Cather.

O Pioneers! Dir. Glenn Jordan. Perf. Jessica Lange, David Strathairn, Anne Heche. 1992. A made-for-TV movie based on the novel by Willa Cather.

Magazines and Journals

Gelfant, Blanche H. "The Forgotten Reaping-Hook: Sex in *My Ántonia*." *American Literature*, 1971: 62–80. Discusses how Jim Burden fits into Cather's sexual themes and male characters, his relationships with Lena and Ántonia, and Cather's representation of the past.

Holmes, Catherine D. "Jim Burden's Lost Worlds: Exile in *My Ántonia*." *Twentieth Century American Literature*, 1999: 336–346. Analyzes conflicts of individuals between the Old World and the New World.

Martin, Terence. "The Drama of Memory in *My Ántonia*." *PMLA*, 1969: 304–311. The author analyzes the role of Jim Burden, the land, the background tensions of American history, and the role of memory in the book.

Seaton, James. "The Prosaic Willa Cather." *The American Scholar*, 1998: 146–158. Develops Cather's ideas regarding romantic love, religion, and family life.

Shaw, Patrick W. "Willa Cather: Emergence and Authorial Revelations." *American Literature*, 1984: 526–540. Explores Cather's views of the past.

Tellefsen, Blythe. "Blood in the Wheat: Willa Cather's *My Ántonia*." *Studies in American Fiction*, 1999: 229–244. Discusses themes from *My Ántonia*.

Send Us Your Favorite Tips

In your quest for knowledge, have you ever experienced that sublime moment when you figure out a trick that saves time or trouble? Perhaps you realized you were taking ten steps to accomplish something that could have taken two. Or you found a little-known workaround that achieved great results. If you've discovered a useful tip that helped you study more effectively and you'd like to share it, the CliffsNotes staff would love to hear from you. Go to our Web site at www.cliffsnotes.com and click the Talk to Us button. If we select your tip, we may publish it as part of CliffsNotes Daily, our exciting, free e-mail newsletter. To find out more or to subscribe to a newsletter, go to www.cliffsnotes.com on the Web.

Index

NOTES

NOTES

1048408536

NOTES

Check Out the All-New CliffsNotes Guides

TECHNOLOGY TOPICS

PERSONAL FINANCE TOPICS

CAREER TOPICS